A CONCISE HISTORY OF BRONZES

A Concise History of BRONZES

GEORGE SAVAGE

209 illustrations
16 in colour

THAMES AND HUDSON · LONDON

PRINTED IN GREAT BRITAIN BY JARROLD AND SONS LIMITED NORWICH

Contents

A DESCRIPTION OF ANCIENT MINING

Surely there is a mine for silver
And a place for gold which they refine.
Iron is taken out of the earth,
And brass is molten out of the stone.
Man setteth an end to darkness,
And searcheth out the furthest bound
The stones of thick darkness and of the shadow of death.
He breaketh open a shaft away from where men sojourn;
They are forgotten of the foot which passeth by;
They hang afar from men, they swing to and fro;
As for the earth, out of it cometh bread:
And underneath it is turned up as it were by fire.
The stones thereof are the place of sapphires,
And it hath dust of gold.
That path no bird of prey knoweth,
Neither has the falcon's eye seen it;
The proud beasts have not trodden it,
Nor hath the fierce lion passed thereby.
He putteth forth his hand upon the flinty rocks;
He overturneth the mountain by the roots.
He cutteth out channels among the rocks;
And his eye seeth every precious thing.
He bindeth the streams that they trickle not;
And the thing that is hid he bringeth forth to light.

THE BOOK OF JOB (CHAPTER XXVIII) *c.* 600 BC

Introduction

'Bronze' is a word derived from the French, who took it, in turn, from the sixteenth-century Italian term 'bronzo', which seems to have come from 'bruno', or brown. To say that it is an alloy of copper and tin would be to oversimplify. In fact bronze is very rarely copper and tin by themselves. Most bronze contains other metals, either added deliberately or present accidentally in the ores from which its constituents were reduced.

To examine all the variations revealed by analysis of the alloys usually termed 'bronze', and the reasons for their adoption, would be much too lengthy to justify inclusion in a book of this nature, but some of the principal additions to the two basic metals will be mentioned hereafter.

Bronze is much more than a metal of practical utility. It is the material of which many of the world's greatest works of art have been made, beginning more than four thousand years ago. It has continued to be the customary medium for metal sculpture, as well as for such architectural features as doors, capitals, sheathing for structural timbers, and roofing. It is only within the last two centuries or so that reasonably efficient substitutes for many of these uses have been available, and bronze has never been superseded for the casting of works of art.

When we look at surviving sculpture from the ancient world we might be forgiven for concluding that stone rather than bronze was the preferred medium, but this is not necessarily true. In certain countries, at certain times, and for many purposes, there is plenty of evidence that bronze was the more highly valued. Its popularity depended on the accessibility of supplies of metal and the technical ability to work it, and, given these, it was nearly always preferred to stone. Corrosion apart, however, bronze possessed the disadvantage that it could be melted down and used again. Phoenician

1. *Kuei*. Food-vessel belonging to the series of ritual vases made in China from the Shang dynasty (*c*. 1523–1028 BC) onwards. This is already in a well-developed style, and primitive vessels have not so far been recovered. It is decorated with a version of the *t'ao t'ieh* mask (p. 106).

traders drove a thriving business in scrap-bronze, and many of the important bronzes which had survived from the ancient world were melted in the holocaust which followed the capture of Constantinople by the Crusaders in 1204, when statues were piled in churches to await consignment to the foundry. Two of the survivals are illustrated elsewhere, the most famous being the four horses of St Mark's in Venice. Bernini robbed the Pantheon of its roof and capitals to make the *baldacchino* in St Peter's, the surplus going to the cannon-founders, and during the Napoleonic Wars bronze statuary of all kinds, as well as church bells, were melted to make cannon. The bronzes of a captured city were always regarded as the prize of the artillery but the age-old custom was put neatly into reverse after Waterloo, when captured French cannon were melted to make the heroic statue of Achilles in Hyde Park as a tribute to the Duke of Wellington from the women of England!

Even so brief an outline of the history of bronze as this one must be put together like a jig-saw from many pieces which can only be made to fit approximately. It must be assembled from the facts of metallurgy, from knowledge of the techniques used to gain and extract the metal from its ores, and from the constituent metals themselves. These facts must be correlated with surviving objects, and with old records. At the end we shall have, in many cases, only a series of inferences, most of which could not in any sense be regarded as final. Much still remains to be discovered, and modern methods enable many bronzes to be saved which would once have been too corroded for preservation.

The first metal to be employed by man was probably gold rather than copper, but copper is also recovered in a metallic form, when

2. Nuraghic bronze figure from Sardinia, so called from their discovery in the *nuraghe* or cone-shaped fortresses of the island. Usually they represent the mother-goddess, warriors, or animals. Eighth to sixth century BC.

3. Statue of Pepi I. Egypt. Sixth dynasty. Last half of the third millennium. This is the earliest bronze statue to be recovered which makes use of the technique of beating copper sheet over wooden formers.

it is termed 'native' copper. Nuggets of several tons in weight have been found in the region of Lake Superior in North America, and copper in this form was at first fairly widely distributed.

The discovery that native copper was malleable – that it could be hammered into shape – did not require a revolution in ways of thought. The reduction of copper from its ores however, which does not necessarily mean raising the temperature to melting-point, was a considerable technical advance, and one probably due to the efforts of the potters. The discovery that the metal could be melted and cast followed, and this demanded a greater development of the resources of early technology, since the temperature needed is much higher than could normally be attained by the pottery kilns of the time, but from this to the production of alloys was no very great step.

Copper and tin ores are often discovered in close association, and sometimes they are combined. For instance, G. M. Davies (*Tin Ores*) refers to a lode of stannite still being worked in China which contains 49·7 per cent of copper and 42·57 per cent of tin, with a little lead and sulphur. This is remarkably close to an analysis of Chinese mirror-bronze, although it bears no relation to the bronze used for most other things.

There are about two hundred ores from which copper may be extracted. Most of them would have yielded far too little to attract the attention of early man, although those yielding about two per cent of copper are worked today. Some ores are indistinguishable from the products of corrosion to be found on excavated bronzes, which are usually referred to as 'patination'. The richest is cuprite, or red oxide of copper. Malachite is a basic carbonate of copper used in powdered form by the Egyptians as a pigment and called *smaragdus medicus* by Pliny, probably because in the form of an eye-paint it was regarded as a protection against ophthalmia. Azurite is a less stable basic carbonate of copper, with a tendency to turn into the more stable malachite. It is blue in colour, and was sometimes used as a substitute for natural ultramarine, the expensive lapis lazuli blue.

The earliest known mines were those of the Egyptians, who sought gold, copper, and turquoise in the Sinai Peninsula in pre-Dynastic times. These, however, were poor, although they were still being worked in Roman times when they were deepened and extended. The principal Egyptian source of copper, especially after the Eighteenth Dynasty, was almost certainly Cyprus, where copper was so abundant that it gave its name to the metal, the Romans at first referring to it as *cyprum*, and only later as *cuprum*. In old alchemical writings the sign ♀ was used to denote copper, and this also represented the planet Venus to whom the island was dedicated. A letter from the King of Cyprus to Akhenaten (1380–1362 BC) refers to the export of copper, saying: 'Whereas I bring thee five hundred [manehs?] of copper as a present unto my brother, I bring them thee. My brother, if the copper is little, let it not rankle in thine heart, for in my country the hand of Nergal [the planet or god, Mars] hath smitten all the people of my country, and the copper working has ceased.'

But if one of the principal sources of copper in the ancient world is known, many others remain obscure, and those from which tin was procured are less certain. The Phoenicians traded with both Spain and Britain for tin, and Britain was known by the name of Cassiterides or the Tin Islands. The metal is still mined in Cornwall, but was formerly much more plentiful. The Phoenicians described the local inhabitants as bearded like goats, subsisting by means of cattle, and leading a wandering life. The trade seems to have been fairly well established by the fifth century, but the possibility that Britain was visited by Greek seamen in search of tin long before this cannot be excluded.

The Phoenicians were excellent bronzeworkers as well as traders, and ancient authors attributed the discovery of copper to Cadmus, son of Agenor the Phoenician. Cadmus was also reputed to have invented many of the useful arts, and Pliny refers to a substance which was called *cadmia*, of which the best came from Cyprus. This seems to have been calamine, a zinc carbonate, and the supposition is made much more likely by its use as a plaster for the itch. Calamine, or *cadmia*, was added to copper and tin to make brass, and, until the seventeenth century of our era, brass was usually made in this way, metallic zinc being first isolated *c.* AD 1000 but remaining a very rare metal. The manufacture of an alloy which can be regarded as brass rather than bronze probably dates from the beginning of the first millennium BC, but zinc ores are often found in close association with those of copper, and it is sometimes difficult to be certain whether zinc was added deliberately.

Until modern times the terms 'bronze' and 'brass' have always been confused with one another, and most ancient languages did not differentiate even between bronze and copper. The classification of metals on strict principles is a relatively modern development, and in earlier times superficial appearance counted for at least as much as the less obvious properties. For this reason the brazen trumpets of the King James's Version of the Old Testament were certainly of bronze, and as late as the end of the seventeenth century AD we find Martin Lister referring to 'brazen' statues and vases when he meant gilded bronze. Since some of the things to which he referred still exist and can be identified there is no doubt of their nature.

It is at present impossible to estimate with any kind of certainty when and where copper and bronze were first used. Certainly Mesopotamia preceded Egypt, and one inscription of Gudea, Governor *c.* 2400 BC of Lagash in the south, refers to the Copper Mountains, which may have been in central or southern Arabia.

4. Copper figure of a god driving a peg into the ground from the foundations of a building. Lagash. Period of the *patesi* or governor, Gudea. *c.* 2400 BC.

There were also important deposits in Persia, in the Caucasus, and in the area of the Caspian and Aral seas, the last once much more fertile than it is today and rich in minerals of all kinds.

The weight of the evidence points to a great increase in the manufacture of objects of bronze in the Mediterranean areas of civilization *c.* 1500 BC, and the reason, since copper was already freely available, must undoubtedly have been more plentiful supplies of tin. The most likely cause of this was that Spanish mines were being opened up by sea-traders, and although the evidence is slight, there is some reason to think that supplies were being brought from Sumatra and Malaya by Phoenician ships. The ancient Tartessos on the Atlantic coast of Spain, probably located on an island at the mouth of the Guadalquivir, is often identified, without certainty, with the Biblical Tarshish. The Book of Ezekiel refers to Tarshish as 'thy merchant by reason of the multitude of all kinds of riches; with silver, iron, tin, and lead they trade in thy fairs'. This, of course, is a comparatively late reference, as the inclusion of iron shows, but all these metals were mined in Spain, at first by the Phoenicians and later by the Romans. Diodorus Siculus, who describes Roman mining techniques in Spain, also refers to deposits of tin in Luisitania (Portugal). When these deposits were first worked is unknown, but Sayce was of the opinion that an inscription of Sargon I (*c.* 2750 BC) referred to Spain under the name of Kugu-ki, or the Tin Land, although this is very doubtful because tin was hardly known as a separate metal at the time.

Lead has always been added to certain bronzes, principally those employed for casting, since it increases the fusibility of the alloy and makes for easier pouring. In combination with tin it forms solder, and alloyed with copper in fairly large quantities it becomes pot-metal, frequently employed for cheap casts needing an easily fused metal. Occasionally lead is found associated with copper ores, and it then occurs as an impurity.

Mercury, used for gilding bronze and copper, was known to the Greeks and is mentioned by Aristotle. This metal is a liquid at ordinary temperatures, and it vaporizes at 357° C. Combined with gold it forms a pasty mass known as an 'amalgam', which can easily

5. This copper figure of a bison, of Sumerian workmanship, was made about 2300 BC and found in the region of Lake Van in eastern Anatolia. It was, no doubt, an object of trade between the two peoples.

be applied to bronze or copper surfaces. When the mercury is volatilized by heating the gold is left firmly adherent to the base metal. The vapour driven off during heating is extremely poisonous. Gilders working on the tomb of Charles the Bold at Bruges were paid forty guilders apiece as compensation for the loss of their teeth, and mercuric gilding (known in France as *doré d'or moulu*) has always been an expensive operation. The process is described by Cellini in his *Treatises*, with advice to the sculptor to leave this work to someone else.

It is necessary to distinguish between bronze which is the result of smelting an ore containing tin and copper in combination, and one made by deliberately adding tin to copper. The period at which copper began to supersede stone for tools and weapons is often referred to as the beginning of the Bronze Age, which is subdivided for convenience into Early, Middle, and Late, but by themselves these terms mean very little. They are only of value chronologically when closely related sites are being discussed. The Copper Age does not exist as a term in general use because, native copper apart, a reasonably pure metal could not be obtained in the early period since there was no reliable way of refining the ores. It is reasonable to say that if by the term Bronze Age we understand the deliberate manufacture of alloys, it did not begin much before 1800 BC.

It was essential to early tool-makers that they should be able to give tools and weapons a good cutting edge. This, sometimes said

6. Chariot found at Strettweg (Austria), one of a number of surviving models of votive chariots made by the nomadic invaders of Europe. First half of the first millennium BC.

to be a lost art, was in fact achieved by cold hammering which consolidated the metal, and this process needed to be followed by annealing to remove the stresses set up by hammering in the metal structure. Bronze, however, was superseded for this purpose by iron and steel which, rusting apart, was very much more efficient for the purpose. The change was forced on early peoples, because warriors equipped with iron swords were almost invariably the victors of any combat. Homer refers to the necessity for pausing to straighten bronze swords.

It is in casting especially that bronze is superior to all other metals. As bronze solidifies it also expands, forcing the metal into every crevice of the mould. Then, in cooling, it contracts slightly, facilitating separation from the mould. It acts in this respect precisely in the same way as plaster of Paris, another popular casting material. A little added lead or zinc improves bronze as a casting metal, and a fairly high tin content is also desirable – say ten per cent at least.

Bronze surfaces are decorated in a number of ways, apart from gilding which was frequently practised. The cutting of linear designs with the aid of a graving-tool (the burin) is almost as old as bronze itself. Inlaying has also been extensively practised. Enamelling, frequently used on bronze and copper bases, requires the addition of coloured glass pastes, subsequently fused by heating, confined by cells scooped into the metal (*champlevé*), or by wires soldered to the surface (*cloisonné*). Bronze casts are finished by chiselling and filing.

The manufacture of bronze and copper in sheet form was an early technical advance, and this led to the embossing of ornament with the aid of punches and hammers and a yielding pitch-block on which the metal was laid. If the decoration is embossed from the back it is usually termed *repoussé*, from the front it is known as 'chasing', a word often misused to describe engraving. Mass-production of embossed ornament was achieved by hammering the sheet into an *intaglio* mould of hardwood.

Sheet-metal cut into an appropriate shape was bent to form vessels, the seams of which were usually soldered and sometimes riveted. 'Raising' vessels was done on an anvil from sheet-metal with a hammer having a hemispherical head. These, usually bowls or dishes, were formed from the centre outwards, often on anvils of special design.

Bowls were also formed by 'spinning', a circular sheet being brought into contact with a revolving former, probably of some kind of hardwood. This is a mass-production technique for making bowls which were then fluted or embossed, but it depends on the existence of a simple lathe. A wood-turning pole-lathe seems to have been in use in Britain during the Late Bronze Age, but the actual date of its invention is extremely uncertain. It is, however, a fairly obvious extension of the potter's wheel, driven by a mechanism based on the bow-drill, and there is no reason why it should not have been devised at an early date.

Casting presupposes a mould, and there are many ways of making them. The earliest was an *intaglio* mould cut into stone. Founders' sand, sometimes bonded with oil or Fuller's earth, is a simple method whereby a prototype is pressed firmly into the sand which retains the form, and into which the metal is poured. Founders' sand has usually been employed for flat ware and reliefs, and the casts need a good deal of cleaning up afterwards. There is no trustworthy evidence of its use before the eighteenth century, although the technique may have been employed by the Chinese for flat weapons before the present era.

Moulds of refractory clay were an early development. The actual melting-point of a really refractory clay is far above that of the metal. The same substance was used to make crucibles in which the metal was melted, and from which it was poured. Plaster of Paris mixed with a refractory substance such as brickdust is also employed, but there is no evidence for its use in the early periods, although plaster as a mould-making material was well known to the Romans. Usually clay moulds were fired, but moulds of unfired clay may have been used, supported against distortion on the outside with sand, but this could only have been for relatively small objects.

The most usual method of casting for fine work was the *cire perdu* or lost wax process, later discussed. Very large statuary was occasionally cast by pouring from the base upwards, fresh mould-sections being added as each part was completed, but most such

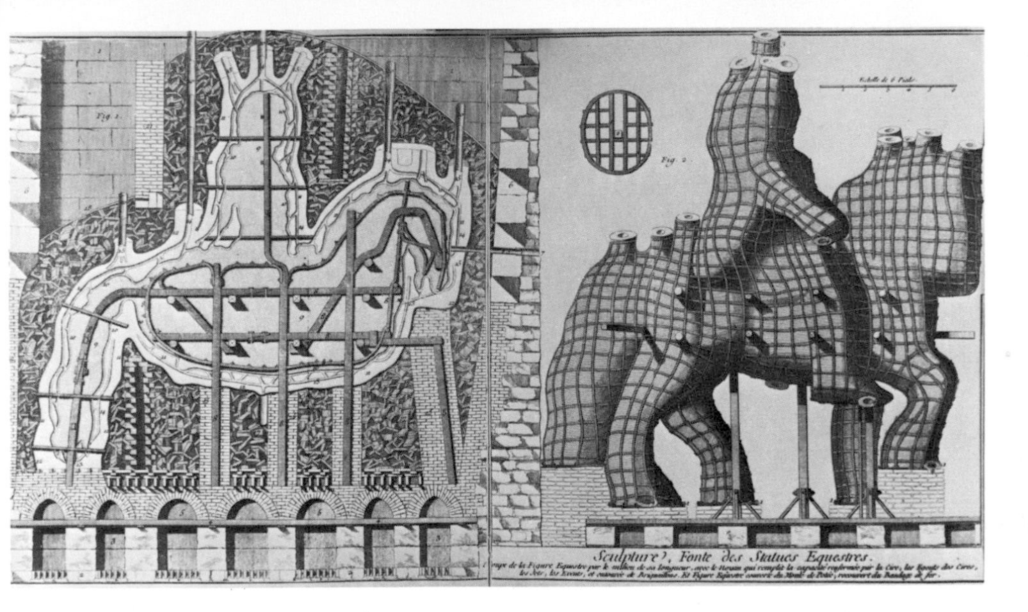

7. Diagram showing pouring-channels and air-vents in the moulds forming a large equestrian statue. Left: section. Right: the moulds in position, strengthened externally and internally with iron rods. After Diderot.

works were cast in sections on the ground and subsequently assembled.

Cellini (*Treatises*) discusses the mystery of making 'great Colossi' in bronze, describing at length a method whereby small models could be copied in a much larger size. He remarks that in colossal work masses of muscle, for instance, appear so huge that they are impossible to comprehend at the distance at which the workman has to stand.

The difficulties of casting large works are discussed by several Renaissance sculptors, of which the description of the casting of Cellini's *Perseus* is the best known, but Michelangelo met similar difficulties, to which he refers in a letter written in January 1507. *Ill. 142*

John Weichard Valvasor refers in 1687 to a method for calculating the quantity of metal required for a large statue. He took part of the wax he proposed to use, carefully weighing it, and then cast a lump of metal from it. 'I thereby computed,' he writes, 'the Proportion of the weight of the Metal and the Wax, and then, observing how many Pounds of Wax I use about the Figure and Channels, I can calculate to a small matter how much Metal I need to melt.'

Casting by the *cire perdu* process is extremely ancient. It is impossible to say where or when it was first used, but it was known to the Sumerians, in the Indus Valley in the Third millenium, and in Egypt by the Eighteenth Dynasty, after 1573 BC. In China it may have been known during the Shang period (1523–1028 BC) although this is uncertain. It can take three forms. In the first a solid model of wax was employed over which a mould of some refractory material (i.e. one capable of resisting great heat) was formed. The wax was melted out and the liquid bronze run in to make a solid cast. The second involved the making of an object in wax modelled over a refractory core. The mould was then formed over the wax. The core was held in position by bronze pins and the wax melted out. Bronze was then poured into the intervening space between mould and core, which were chipped away with chisels to leave a hollow cast. Both these methods involved the destruction of the original model. A third method, which first came into use among the Greeks and was extensively employed thereafter, required a mould formed over an original model which might be either in wood or stone, and sometimes of clay or plaster. The surface of the mould, after removal of the prototype was then covered with a layer of wax and filled with a core of refractory material. The wax could then be melted out as before, and the bronze poured in. This preserved the model for later use, and it enabled casts to be multiplied from the same original work. This process required a considerable advance in the making of moulds, which had to be piece-moulds instead of waste-moulds, since the mould-sections had to be removed from an original which was not always plastic.

Wax-modelling for decorative purposes, quite apart from its use for bronze-casting, existed at least by the sixth century, since Anacreon addressed an ode to a Cupid modelled in wax, and, according to Pliny, a sculptor of the fourth century, Lysistratus, cast figures and portraits of wax in moulds. The best description of the process of casting by the lost wax process is to be found in Cellini's *Memoirs*, where he describes the casting of his *Perseus*.

The lost wax technique, especially the third variety, continued to be the principal method employed for forming objects of bronze until the nineteenth century, when the process of electrotyping was devised. This gives a mechanical reproduction of an original model by which an electric current is used to take particles of metal from a bar suspended in an electrolytic solution, depositing them on the face of the mould until the required thickness has been built up. Very thin and accurate facsimiles can be attained in this way, and the process has been employed to produce replicas of old bronzes for decorative purposes.

A word in general could well be said at this point on the subject of style in bronzework as the product of technique.

A stone statue is imprisoned inside a block of stone, to be liberated by taking away the material with chisels, punches, and abrasives. Metal statuary, whatever the size, is not usually formed by reducing the volume of the material, but by adding to it. Most original models are made in a plastic substance such as clay or wax, although occasionally moulds taken directly from a wood or stone prototype occur. Some bronze objects are formed by direct hammering, but here the material is forced into shape. Nothing is taken away, except perhaps by filing. The differences in style dictated by the material – stone, wood, or bronze – are therefore usually obvious.

Bronzes, especially the later varieties, can also be separated into sculptor's work and goldsmith's work. Objects in the former category are conceived in broad planes and masses, and although casting blemishes were cleaned off by chiselling and filing, very few significant additions or alterations were made after casting. In the second case, however, a great deal of work was done afterwards by chiselling, filing, and engraving, in the same way as the precious metals were treated by the goldsmith. This is especially to be seen in eighteenth-century France, where bronzes were handed for finishing to a *ciseleur* or chiseller, who not only cleaned up the rough cast but often added to the ornament, but it occurs at all periods. Bronzes finished in the manner of the goldsmith may often be recognized by the amount of finely detailed ornament cut in after the actual work of casting had been completed.

Copper alloys corrode readily, and in the case of bronze this corrosion may proceed to a point where the tin separates from the copper. Usually, however, the effects of corrosion are more limited in extent and do not penetrate very much below the surface. Under the name of *patina* they are a much-prized quality of old bronze.

Untouched patination is desirable for several reasons, chief among them being that if these products of corrosion are removed we are left with something like the original colour, but with a corroded surface which is rarely an improvement. To remove patination also destroys what is often the best evidence of antiquity, and this is sometimes the most reliable way of separating genuine objects from spurious. Patination is sometimes removed to reveal inlaying or an inscription, but this is specialized work.

The three common ores of copper, cuprite, malachite, and azurite, also occur as products of corrosion. Of the three the reddish-brown cuprite is probably the most important if not the most spectacular. When bronze is first cast a normal alloy has a rich golden colour, which is lighter if zinc is present in appreciable quantities, and inclined to be greyish-blue if there is overmuch lead. The ordinary golden-brown will eventually turn first a reddish-brown, then brown, and finally a dark brown. Very often, however, a light green sulphate will form on the surface.

Bronzes which have been buried corrode much more seriously, and this causes the formation of products which are variable in colour – several shades of green, blue, brown, and even black.

Dr Plenderleith suggests that all genuine patina on excavated bronze has an underlying foundation of cuprite, even when the subsequent layers are green or blue, and this seems to be a generalization with a good foundation.

When hard and even some kinds of patination will take a fairly good polish, and certain bronzes which have been lying under water for long periods of time became covered with a smooth, hard olive-green surface which is almost enamel-like in appearance. This is sometimes called 'water'-patination. A black patination often forms on bronzes which contain a high percentage of tin, and the presence of silver in the alloy has the same effect.

8. Bronze head of a Pharaoh wearing a warrior's helmet. Cast in a single mould, this head was at one time thought to be a portrait of Rameses II, but it is now regarded as later. *c.* 400 BC.

When patination is relatively soft and porous, and the object has been buried in a saline soil, it tends to retain salts which then form light green spots, moist and pasty in a humid atmosphere, and dry and powdery in one which is relatively free from moisture. This has been termed 'bronze disease' or, sensationally, 'bronze cancer', but it can usually be checked or subdued by prolonged immersion in distilled water, although more specialist treatment is sometimes needed.

Corrosion is rarely uniform over the whole surface. Local variations in soil-conditions cause it to be variegated, differing in extent and depth. The same piece may have areas of cuprite, malachite, and blue azurite, although the last is unusual since it tends to revert to the more stable malachite. Undoubtedly the most colourful examples of bronze patination are to be found among the excavated vessels of China.

It has been the custom from very early times to impart colour to the surface of bronze in a variety of ways, apart from variations in the alloying metals employed. Surface treatment of this kind has little effect on the patination of excavated specimens, and it survives principally among those things which have remained above ground.

It is difficult to imitate air-patination convincingly, but it is often attempted with chemical solutions termed 'pickles'. 'Pickled' bronzes are not invariably spurious. It was a very common practice among nineteenth-century collectors and even museum curators to clean off original patination when it was not to their taste, and to replace it with another colour. The agents recommended ranged from the obvious sal ammoniac, known to the Romans, to smoking, with green willow twigs and old shoes as fuel.

CHAPTER ONE

Bronzeworkers of the ancient world

We cannot say when metals in their native form were first used; we can only guess when and where they were first smelted. It is possible, in these days, to place the beginning of a settled agricultural way of life to about nine thousand years ago, and discoveries yet to be made may push this date still further back. We cannot entirely exclude the chance of settlements in places later made untenable by drastic climatic changes of the kind which seem to have taken place in Siberia, an area over which hangs a big question-mark.

When people speaking the Sumerian language first began to inhabit the valleys of the Euphrates and the Tigris pottery was their principal manufacture, but Sir Leonard Woolley discovered objects of copper in the tomb of Queen Shub-ad at Ur – vessels, a relief of two lions, and a much-decayed model of a ship of a kind similar to the boats in use to this day on the lower reaches of the Euphrates. These belong to a period shortly after 3000 BC, but the competence of the workmanship suggests that a tradition of metalworking was well established.

Technically Lower Mesopotamia was in advance of Egypt. The wheel, for instance, was invented by *c.* 3000 BC, but it seems not to have reached Egypt before *c.* 1800 BC with the invasion of the nomadic Hyksos. It is, of course, possible to make a wheeled cart without metals, but such a vehicle would have been inefficient and heavy to pull, and certainly unsuitable for horse traction.

The part played in the dissemination of the art of metalworking by nomadic tribes wandering between the plains of Russia in the west and the Ordos Desert in the east deserves especial attention. Pressure in the east resulting from expansion of a particular group forced the remainder to the west, and in their passage they attacked centres of early civilization, sometimes remaining to become part of the indigenous population, or to found city-states of their own.

The outcome of these descents on the growing focal points of civilization depended largely on two factors – the development of weapons equal or superior to those of opponents, and the evolution of tactics by which the weapons could be efficiently deployed. The city-dwellers defended themselves with weapons which may not always have been superior, but they were able to erect permanent defensive walls and earthworks. Their own most successful contribution to the art of war, however, was the evolution of disciplined movement which countered nomadic mobility. Nevertheless, as Darius was later to discover in his attack on the Scythians, it was virtually impossible to defeat a nomadic people who had room to manœuvre.

Nomadic pressures in Mesopotamia came from the north, where large deposits of ores existed which, in part, supplied the metalworkers of the south. The nomads wandered through eastern Iran, round the northern borders of Mesopotamia, and onwards into

9. Lion formed from bronze sheet. From the Temple of Dagon at Mari on the west bank of the Euphrates. The inhabitants were the Biblical Amorites – the Amurru. *c.* 2255–2150 BC.

10. Copper panel forming part of a Sumerian shrine. Dating from about 2900 BC it is evidence of a people well advanced in metalworking techniques who employed sheet copper extensively in the decoration of interiors.

Anatolia and central Europe. About 2100 BC they overwhelmed the early settlement at Troy, descended into Greece, and pushed on into the Balkans. Others, the Slavs, Germans, and Celts, later fanned out into the west European plains. The Semitic nomads, who probably came from Arabia, were in contact with the civilizations of both Mesopotamia and Egypt, and as the Israelites they took fire and sword to the ancient settlements of Palestine, to Jericho which existed by about 6800 BC, and to Hazor founded in 2100 BC.

There is evidence of an advanced kind of metalworking in the Caucasus, an area well known for its deposits of copper both in the ancient world and in sixteenth-century England. In AD 1557 a letter written by English merchants to their Russian agents refers to 'the great plentie of copper in the Emperour's dominion'. A barrow excavated at Maikop, fifty miles inland from the Black Sea and dating from about 2500 BC, contained copper tools of excellent workmanship, as well as silver vessels decorated in styles associated with the nomads.

Hallstatt in Austria, in the valley of the Danube and not far from Salzburg, is situated in an area rich in metallic deposits of all kinds,

11 (*left*). Ewer inlaid with coral and enamel found in the Moselle area. Celtic. La Tène style. Enamelling is an especially advanced technical achievement for which the Celts were noted.

12. Bronze shield in the La Tène style. *c.* 200 BC. The geometric ornament based on compass-work is often associated with nomadic craftsmen. It is a motif which returned to Europe in the eleventh century of our era with the rise of the Gothic style.

and it has proved extremely rich in bronze objects of fine workmanship, both embossed and chiselled, the earliest of which date to *c.* 1000 BC. Horse-bits and bridles are among the objects recovered. The Celts were metalworkers of great skill who particularly excelled in the use of bronze. The relatively late Iron Age settlement of La Tène, at the eastern end of Lake Neuchâtel in Switzerland, has yielded objects decorated in an eastern European style, including horse-bits, tools, weapons, and vessels such as the impressive ewer shown here. *Ill. 11*

When the Phoenicians reached the Tin Islands, as Britain was then called, they found the inhabitants already acquainted with bronze, which first appears *c.* 1800 BC at the same time as the erection of Stonehenge. The products of Middle European copper-mines were an article of trade by 2000 BC and the casting of bronze was well known in Scandinavia by *c.* 1500 BC. A remarkable instance of the metalwork of the period is the Sun Chariot, found at Trundholm, with the sun's disc of gold. The large serpentine trumpet, the *lur*, essentially Danish, was cast by the lost wax process.

Ill. 13

The island of Sardinia was inhabited by a community well acquainted with bronzeworking, although there were hardly any supplies of copper and none of tin. The Sardinians, therefore, must have been supplied by sea with ingots and scrap-bronze. Copper ingots weighing about four pounds have been discovered, and the island is noted for some curious bronze figures.

13. The Sun Chariot from Trundholm. First half of the first millennium BC. The worship of the sun was widespread among the nomads, and the horse held a significant place in their beliefs. The association of the two survived in the myth of the sun chariot of Apollo.

14. Bull, formerly a temple ornament, of copper over a core of bitumen. Sumeria. Al 'Ubaid. First half of the third millennium BC. The bull is one of the most frequent and widespread of ancient decorative motifs.

Although the metal industry of each locality took shape according to local circumstances and in response to local needs, there was a considerable trade in scrap-bronze, for which reason analyses are not always helpful. The resourceful Phoenicians no doubt purchased old statues and structural fittings, as well as outworn pots and pans, for remelting.

The bronzesmith himself was often a travelling craftsman, regarded with superstitious awe and veneration. Even today among primitive peoples the smith is still credited with magical powers. During the Bronze Age he moved from place to place with the tools of his trade and a portable forge, making new implements from ingots or refurbishing old ones. His work was accompanied by traditional rites and ceremonies. No doubt smiths were organized into guilds, taking wives from each other's families, and handing down their craft secrets. As a privileged caste they wandered without fear, and had a fire god as their patron. In Roman days the god Hephaistos or Vulcan was a smith who manifested himself in the burning gases of volcanoes, with a smithy on Olympus or Aetna where he was assisted by one-eyed Cyclopes to make armour and ornaments of metal.

Typical of the nomadic metalworkers were those inhabiting the northern part of the Iranian province of Luristan from about the fourteenth to the sixth century BC. Horse-bits, and harness and chariot-fittings, are among the most frequent survivals, but tools and weapons, including some fine battle-axes, are also known. A bronze of unknown purpose is the so-called standard, representing a hero, perhaps Gilgamesh, wrestling with two animals, one on either side. The motif however is not confined to Luristan bronzes, but is also found much further west. Fertility goddesses probably represented Astarte, 'the abomination of the Sidonians', who is synonomous with Ishtar and Aphrodite.

Some Luristan bronzes show distinct affinities with the nomadic bronzes of the Ordos Desert, which are remarkable for a lively rendering of animal subjects, a common nomadic *motif*. These are, in turn, related to Scythian animal bronzes ranging from perhaps the seventh century BC to the second century AD. That all had a common origin in the central Asiatic steppe can hardly be doubted, and they affected Chinese animal representations certainly by about the fourth century BC and perhaps much earlier.

The Sumerians established a commercial civilization in Mesopotamia which was organized on almost modern lines; merchants rented offices from which they transacted business and were able to use a kind of banking system for payments abroad. Caravans plied regularly between cities, and it is even probable that trading expeditions reached central Europe, where manufactured goods, including copper and bronze, were exchanged for raw materials. Technically, even in 2700 BC, their metalwork was advanced, and they employed sheet copper for sheathing beams and pillars. The same sheet copper hammered against a yielding block of bitumen was a customary technique for architectural ornament. The bitumen was rarely removed.

Ill. 10

But Mesopotamia became a cockpit, and the Babylonians, Assyrians, Mitanni, Hittites, and Egyptians struggled for supremacy. Both the Babylonians and the Assyrians were accomplished metalworkers, and some later Persian stone-carving suggests the influence of bronze statuary which no longer exists. By the time of Sennacherib (705–681 BC) very large objects were being cast. An inscription of this period records that 'I, Sennacherib, achieved the casting of colossal bronze lions, open at the knees, which no King before me had done. Over great posts and palm-trunks I built a clay mould for twelve colossal lions together with twelve colossal bulls . . . and poured bronze therein as in casting half-shekel pieces.' There is no reason to distrust the term 'colossal' – surviving stone sculpture of the period could certainly be thus called – although the work may have been cast in sections, since there is a limit to the size of the crucible which could be manhandled into position for pouring.

The description seems to suggest that the figures of lions and bulls were part of a 'Brazen Sea' of a kind commonly to be found before the temples of the region. The best known of these was the Brazen Sea of Solomon, of which a description survives in the Book of Kings. With the aid of a Phoenician artificer from Tyre Solomon 'cast a Brazen Sea' with a laver ten feet in diameter, round which 'stood twelve oxen that looked to the four winds of heaven'. On these the laver rested. This Sea is minutely described by Josephus,

15. A reconstruction of the courtyard of Solomon's Temple showing the Brazen Sea and the wheeled laver, the latter a movable basin. The Brazen Sea contained about 9,000 gallons of water. Based on the descriptions of the Bible and Josephus. After Perrot and Chipiez.

who also writes of the numerous 'brazen' altar-vessels, as well as the great seven-branched candelabrum of the Temple, now known only from its appearance in sculptured form on the Arch of Titus, the original being lost in the Tiber during the fourth century AD.

Ill. 15 A reconstruction of the Sea is illustrated here. Evidence that the Old Testament description, and that of Josephus, is not exaggerated is only now coming to light with excavations at Ezion-Geber at the head of the Gulf of Aqabah, where, in Solomon's time, there were ore refineries, mainly handling copper, which were capable of dealing with very large quantities, the furnaces being provided with an ingenious forced-draught system.

When Layard excavated the site of Nimrûd he found bronze cauldrons thirty inches in diameter with lions' and bulls' feet not far away, probably part of the loot of the Palace of Ashurnasirpal II taken by Sargon II (722–705 BC). Two circular vessels of flattened form had a diameter of six feet and a depth of two feet. Some of the bronzes were of Phoenician workmanship, evidence of the extent of their trade, while others – friezes of hunting scenes, combats between men and lions, gazelles, stags, wild goats, and griffins – are to some extent more familiar from 'Orientalizing' Greek work. The proportion of copper to tin was nine to one. An interesting technical development was to be found in the foreleg of a bull, perhaps a furniture-mount, cast over an iron core, a method sometimes employed by the Egyptians in the late Dynastic period.

Perhaps the earliest surviving example of bronze sheathing for doors occurs in a remarkable series of friezes which once adorned wooden gates of the Palace of Shalmaneser III, and commemorated *Ill. 16* his defeat of a combined army of Hittites and Syrians. In the words of a contemporary inscription, he 'washed his weapons in the sea, and took in tribute silver, gold, tin, and vessels of copper'. Much use of bronze for architectural purposes is evident at the time – for example, the pillars of Solomon's Temple. Assyrian pillars were adorned on the exterior with a bronze semblance of the palm-trunk, the terminals being capitals of the same metal.

To the east of Mesopotamia lay the country inhabited by former nomadic tribes which had settled permanently – the Medes and the

16. Detail of a hinge from the bronze gates of Shalmaneser III of Assyria. Made about 838 BC. This is the earliest surviving specimen of a bronze door in reasonably complete state. The ornament records Shalmaneser's campaigns and depicts weapons and military equipment.

Persians. The Medes captured Nineveh in 606 BC. Babylon fell to Darius the Mede, general of Cyrus the Great (d. 528) in 539 BC. The account of its fall is confused, but descriptions of Babylon at the height of its prosperity are given both by Herodotus and Diodorus Siculus. Herodotus refers to brazen portrait statues, and between the two halves of the city, separated by the river, ran a tunnel with bronze gates at either end. The famous golden statues which stood on top of the Temple of Jupiter (Belus) were probably of gilded bronze if the estimate of the weight made by Herodotus is to be trusted.

The influence of Assyria is to be noticed in a good deal of Iranian art, and although no large bronzes have been recovered it is probable that they existed. The Persians were skilled metalworkers, and notable examples of animal sculpture in bronze have been found at Persepolis and Susa. They were skilful casters of plaques and small sculpture in the round, carefully finished by chiselling and engraving. Little is known of metalwork under the Seleucid and Parthian kings, and a distinctively Persian style was not again evident until the rise of the Sassanian kings in the third century AD.

The pre-Dynastic Egyptians were by no means uncivilized or primitive. The term means little more than an absence of information about their rulers. The exploitation of the copper, malachite, and turquoise deposits of the Sinai Peninsula started in pre-Dynastic times, although they later turned to the eastern desert for supplies of copper, as well as to the south. Trading relations with Crete had already been established before historic times. It is evident that metalworking was understood and practised fairly widely before 3000 BC, and by the close of the Dynastic period known as the Old Kingdom hinges, bowls, vessels, weapons, nails, and many objects of everyday utility were being made in copper.

Near the end of the Sixth Dynasty (*c.* 2300 BC) the well known statues of King Pepi I accompanied by his son were made. The technique is extremely advanced for its period. Since true bronze was rare in Egypt at the time these were at first thought to be of copper, but an analysis made in 1907 revealed 6·5 per cent of tin. Maspero, who described the statue of the King in 1910, says that the

Ill. 3

17. Door-hinge from a temple or shrine. Egypt. Twenty-fifth dynasty. *c.* 725 BC. Ancient records amply testify to the extensive use throughout the ancient world of bronze and copper for architectural purposes.

torso, arms, and legs were formed of plates beaten into shape over wooden formers and riveted and welded at the joints without soldering. The face, hands, and feet were cast. The kilt, now missing, may have been of gold or electrum (an alloy of silver and gold). The eyes are inlaid with what seems to be enamel, and the headdress with lapis lazuli or a blue glazed material similar to that which covered the 'faience' figures.

The Old Kingdom persisted until *c.* 2400 BC. The Middle Kingdom (2300–*c.* 1580 BC) was a period at the end of which, during the Fifteenth and Sixteenth Dynasties, Egypt was ruled by the nomadic invaders called Hyksos by Josephus who entered Egypt by way of the Sinai Peninsula. These people probably introduced the chariot, and they improved Egyptian metalworking techniques. It is clear that the Hyksos exhibited all the characteristics of nomadic raiders further north, possessing a fairly advanced metal technology and wheeled vehicles. During their occupation bronze seems to have become much more plentiful in Egypt, presupposing access to more plentiful supplies of tin which had previously been a rare metal.

18. The goddess Isis carrying the infant Harpocrates (Horus), the head-dress representing the cow-horns (an animal sacred to her) and the solar disc. Egypt. *c.* 700 BC.

19 (*right*). The goddess Bast is usually represented with the head of a cat, holding a sistrum in one hand and an aegis in the other. Egypt.

20 (*far right*). Knûm, a Nile god who formed the Universe from the mud of the Nile and shaped man on the potter's wheel. He is usually depicted with the head of a ram. Egypt. Ptolemaic.

The Hyksos were finally expelled *c.* 1580 BC, and Egyptian military power which grew out of the struggle was developed and extended. The army was put on a better organized and more disciplined footing and provided with improved weapons. Military adventures followed, Egyptian armies invading Palestine and Syria and ultimately reaching as far as the upper waters of the Euphrates. In the reign of Amenhotep III Mesopotamia itself fell under Egyptian influence. Military expansion was accompanied by increased trade, and Egypt became a large metal importer, buying lead, copper, and tin in ingot form from Cyprus and the east. Letters to Akhenaten (1380–1362 BC) from the King of Cyprus, found at Tell-el-Amarna, refer to tributes of copper, and it has even been suggested that the Egyptians traded for copper with the Danubian countries.

Military expansion was renewed in the Nineteenth Dynasty, although the movement received a severe check with the Battle of Kadesh, when, despite claims of complete victory, the Egyptians under Rameses II (1296–1229 BC) seem to have failed to force a decision, and Syria was perforce divided between them and their

21. Censer with a falcon- or hawk-head terminal. Egypt. 850 BC.

Hittite opponents. Towards the end of the same century an invasion from Libya was supported by sea-raiders who harassed the eastern Mediterranean coasts generally towards the end of the second millennium BC.

These sea-raiders, who have been tentatively identified with the Sardinians, the inhabitants of Sicily, and the Etruscans, were nomads who had taken to the sea, and one branch, the Philistines, may have come from Crete. They settled in Palestine, and appear to have been skilful metalworkers who overran a great deal of the country. They seem either to have assimilated or extirpated the native smiths by the time of Saul, since we find in the Book of Samuel, 'Now there was no smith to be found throughout the Land of Israel.' The armour of the Philistine leader, Goliath, is described in detail by the same source – a helmet of 'brass', a coat of mail (probably a cuirass is intended), greaves, and a shield (target) of 'brass'. These sea-raiders brought with them the use of iron, and the same source refers to Goliath's spear-head, which 'weighed six hundred shekels of iron', perhaps about twelve pounds which is not unreasonable for a very strong man. The lack of metalworkers among the Israelites is emphasized by David's armament – a sling, and the nomadic origin of the Philistines is evident in the passage which reads, 'So the Philistines were subdued, and came no more to the coasts of Israel.'

Both David and Solomon were powerful enough to prevent the traditional use of their territory as a marshalling ground for forces from east and west, and to this the revival of metalworking on a large scale under Solomon no doubt contributed, but after Solomon's death Sheshank I (947–925 BC) of the Twenty-second Dynasty attacked Jerusalem with twelve hundred chariots, carrying off the gold shields and brazen vessels of the Temple.

After this Egypt became progressively weaker and the Assyrians grew bolder, invading Israel and capturing Phoenician cities. In 670 BC they invaded Egypt itself, and held the country until the revival of the Saïte period (645–525 BC), during which many of the surviving small bronzes were made, and after which very little good bronzework was done.

Although sheet copper was being cut out and fashioned into vessels, with cast spouts riveted into position, in the First Dynasty, and by the Third Dynasty the spouts were being brazed, bronze did not come into common use before the Eighteenth Dynasty of the

22. An ibis, sacred to Thoth, who is sometimes depicted with an ibis head. Like Ra, Thoth existed from the beginning of time, and is represented wearing the lunar crescent and disc. Egypt. Saïte-Ptolemaic period.

New Kingdom. The statue of Pepi I is, up to the present time, an almost isolated instance of the early use of true bronze, and bronze sculpture largely dates from the Twentieth Dynasty. Most specimens are small since tin was always scarce.

There is little difference in the pose of Egyptian statuary in any material before the Saïte period. Gods and goddesses are formally seated, the legs together. Most standing figures have the left leg advanced and the arms close to the sides. Completely nude figures are unusual, the females wearing a long skirt from waist to ankle and the males a short kilt with the pleats formally arranged. Head-dresses range from the simple wig to elaborate tall crowns indicative of the status of the wearer. Traces of gold-leaf can sometimes be detected on bronzes, and inlaying with gold, silver, and electrum was practised. Bronzes are more lifelike than stone-carvings, and during the Saïte period much greater freedom of pose is often to be observed. Kneeling figures offering sacrifices, small figures of worshippers, and so on, are no longer in the traditional form. Groups of figures on a common base have also been found, but these are rare.

Relatively, animal bronzes abound, and animals were a favourite subject with the Egyptian craftsman – the small ichneumon, slayer of serpents; the uraeus or hooded cobra; the jackal (Anubis); the ibis (one of the forms of Thoth); the cat, sacred to Bast; and many others. The cat was an especial favourite, accompanying its master on hunting expeditions and perhaps even trained to retrieve small birds. Diodorus Siculus was eye-witness of an attack by a crowd on a Roman legionary who had accidentally killed a cat, and it is amusing to recall that a pet-name for cats was Mauu. The Chinese gave the name Mao to their cats. Most of the finer bronzes are in the customary seated position, but delightful small groups of cats with kittens exist. Some wear a gold earring.

Ills. 22, 23

23. Model of a cat, sacred to Bast. The cat, an especially favoured pet, appears in Egyptian art in many forms, of which this is perhaps the most familiar. Egypt. Roman period.

During the Roman period decorative bronzes deteriorated in quality, and pot-metal (an alloy of copper and lead) was used for inferior work.

The Hittites earlier mentioned controlled rich mines of copper, lead, and silver in their Anatolian homeland, and they appear to have possessed the secret of working iron before any of the other ancient peoples. It was to this no doubt that they owed their military success.

The Phoenicians were exceptionally skilled bronzeworkers. Perhaps originally from the region of the Persian Gulf, they had settled on the coasts of Palestine as sea-traders by 1200 BC, with *entrepôts* at Tyre and Sidon. The work of the Sidonians was especially esteemed in the ancient world, and some surviving works in bronze and silver frequently show strong Egyptian and Assyrian influence, often to the point of being frank copies. These things were probably made as articles of commerce and sold in countries other than those which inspired them. A Phoenician silver bowl copying Egyptian work, for instance, has been excavated in Italy. Many surviving bronze figures which can be assigned to the Phoenicians are crude and not of very good quality, but this is probably due to the fact that they were made in large quantities for export.

The Phoenicians colonized North Africa, founding the city of Carthage in 853 BC, and from here they journeyed to Spain, where they founded the city of Gades on the site of the modern Cadiz. This no doubt acted as the depôt from which they exploited the mineral riches of the Iberian Peninsula.

Although this is a brief and lacunary outline of the development of the art of bronze in the ancient world, it helps in some measure to form a picture of the part played by this metal in fostering the growth of the great civilizations of the past. Much remains to be discovered, and many conjectures will eventually have to be discarded. The following chapter will help to enlarge the picture, since we are entering a period about which more is known.

CHAPTER TWO

Bronzes of the Classical world

Greek bronzes fall into two categories – cast work and hammered. The making of flat bronze sheets suitable for hammering into shape was introduced into the Greek mainland at an early date, probably from Crete or Egypt. Vessels especially were made in this way. Perhaps the most remarkable surviving specimen is the massive vase found at Vix and now in the Museum at Châtillon-sur-Seine, which is about five feet in height with a weight of 300 pounds.

Ills. 27, 28

Sheet-metal was also employed in the making of statuary in the Egyptian manner to which reference has already been made in discussing the statue of Pepi I. The sections were formed by hammering sheets over wooden formers, which were attached to each other by rivets. This early technique had been abandoned by the seventh century BC, although it survived in chryselephantine work, of which the most famous example was the *Olympian Zeus* which Phidias plated with gold, bronze, and ivory. This, forty-five feet in height, was transported to Constantinople, where it was destroyed by fire in AD 475. Known from its representations on coins, however, it has since inspired relatively modern work, for example a nineteenth-century statue of Washington by Greenough. According to Pausanias, Learchus of Rhegium made a large statue of Zeus which was wrought in sections and assembled *c.* 720 BC.

24. Belonging to the same period as statuary made from sheet bronze are small figures hammered and cut from bronze ingots, such as the horse shown here. Greek. *c.* 750 BC.

25. Bronze dagger-blade inlaid with gold, silver and niello, from Mycenae. This is in an excellent state of preservation. Usually the conjunction of different metals in this way leads to much more rapid corrosion of an irretrievable kind than the use of simple copper or bronze.

Solid casting was known in Crete at a comparatively early date, and implements of copper have been found in the island which were probably made soon after 3000 BC. True bronze was known about 2300 BC. The copper used in Crete no doubt came from Cyprus, which was under Cretan domination. Apart from objects of bronze recovered by excavation, the pottery of the period is in some cases an excellent guide to bronze vessels otherwise lost, some of it copying the seams and rivets of metal prototypes.

The Cretans, however, were not especially skilled in bronze statuary, which largely developed on the mainland. The Mycenaeans were much influenced by Cretan craftsmen, and the art of inlaying bronze with gold was, no doubt, learned from this source.

From Olympia, probably inspired by migrating Cretan craftsmen, have come some very early animals of sheet bronze, cut out in a form resembling the animal's hide and bent round until they could be stood on their legs. Most of these, as well as animals and human figures hammered from ingots, seem to have been intended as

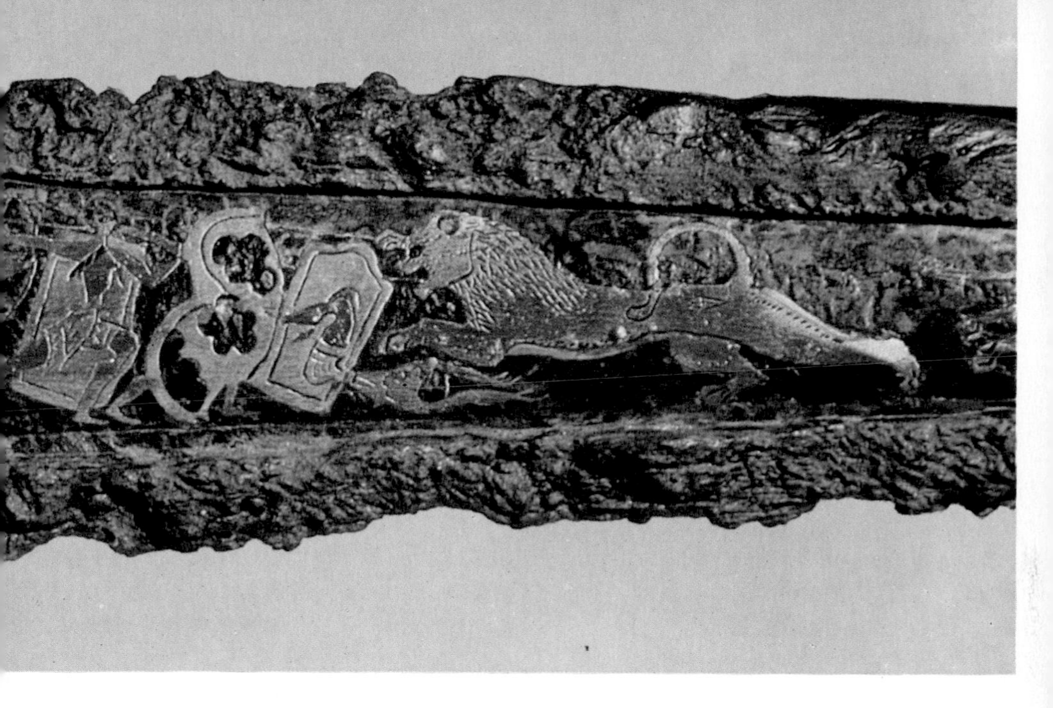

votive offerings, since they occur especially in the vicinity of temples.

Solid casting could only be used for small figures since bronze was both scarce and costly, and much in demand for tools and weapons as well as for pots and pans and armour, but no attempt seems to have been made for a considerable period to save metal by employing a core. Perhaps the largest known solid casting, dating from the sixth century, is forty-two centimetres in height.

Traditionally the first to cast statues instead of building them from preformed hammered sections were Rhoecus, Telecles, and Theodorus of Samos in the middle of the seventh century BC. The last two named are said by Diodorus Siculus to have been sons of Rhoecus. They are also said to have learned their art in Egypt. Pliny writes of Theodorus 'that he cast a bronze statue of himself holding in one hand a file and in the other a quadriga [a four-horse chariot] of such small dimensions that a fly might cover it with his wings', which is typical of the legends which had gathered round the names of some of these early craftsmen by the first century AD.

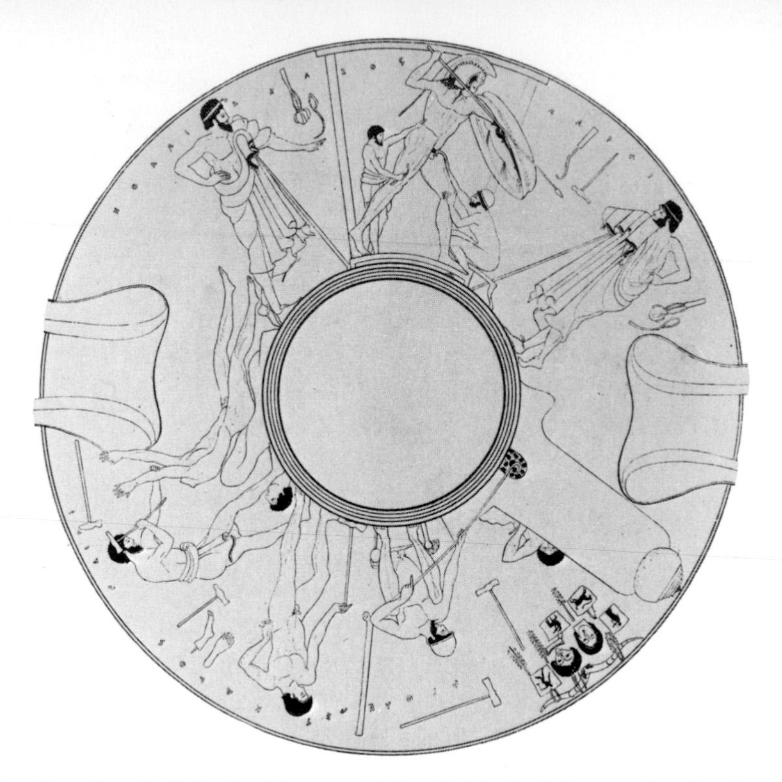

26. Exterior of a *kylix* (a wide cup with handles) in Red-figure style painted with scenes inside a bronze-foundry. Greek. Fifth century BC. From Vulci, and now in Berlin. After Schreiber.

27, 28 (*right*). Bronze *krater* of superb workmanship, nearly five feet in height. Probably Greek, later sixth century BC. Found at Vix, near La Rochelle in France, and no doubt brought by sea.

Large statuary, however, was undoubtedly cast in sections and fitted together afterwards. Not only is this certain from surviving *Ill. 26* examples, but a well known cup at Berlin depicts the interior of a sculptor's workshop with parts of figures hanging on the wall ready for assembly, and it shows a male figure complete but for the head which lies beside it. Among the tools hanging on the wall are large hammers and a toothed saw. To one side, metal is being melted to make fresh casts. The other part of the cup depicts completed statuary being finished with chisels and scrapers.

29. Banqueter reclining on a couch. Greek. Probably from the Peloponnese. Later sixth century B C. The same subject is to be found in Etruscan art.

30. Figure of a girl running. Greek. 500 B C. A very lively little figure for so early a period.

31. Solid cast-bronze statuette of a warrior on horseback. Greek. *c.* 550 B C.

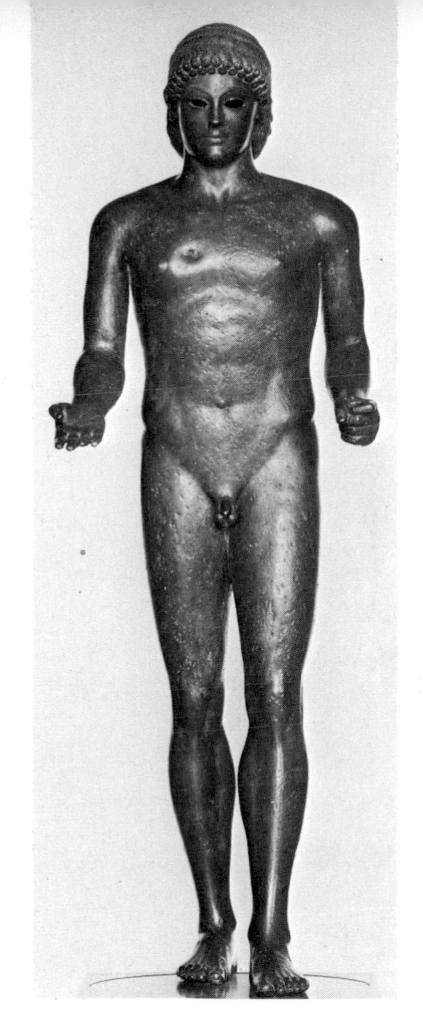

32. *The Piombino Apollo*. Greek. *c*. 500 BC. It represents the transition between the Archaic style and later more natural representation. It was found in the sea near Piombino.

The lost wax technique was probably being employed both for solid and hollow casts by the seventh century BC, although it has been suggested that wooden figures were used as a base instead of those of wax. This is doubtful, but carved wood figures were commonly to be found in temples at least until 500 BC, after which they were replaced by those of stone and bronze. A life-size bronze Apollo discovered a few years ago on the Piraeus at Athens still had its clay core and an armature of iron, which gives some indication of the customary technique.

33. Medieval engraving of Helios, the sun god, known as the Colossus of Rhodes. This shows its traditional form, but the foundations were discovered in the nineteenth century, and the story that it bestrode the harbour entrance is a romantic fiction. It was finally broken up for scrap-metal by the Saracens in the eighth century AD

That statues of heroic size and colossi were cast in sections is certain. Notable among the latter was the statue of Helios at Rhodes, the so-called Colossos, 120 feet in height and one of the Seven Wonders of the ancient world. A conjectural medieval restoration, which is undoubtedly largely inaccurate, is illustrated. According to Pliny this statue, constructed by Charos in the second century BC, lay prone in his day, and was so big that few men could encircle the thumb with their arms, while the interior of the limbs appeared like vast caverns. By tradition it was cast piecemeal from the feet upwards, with masses of rock to form a core, but this is unlikely, and it was probably cast on the ground in sections and afterwards assembled. The only work now existing which is comparable in size is the Statue of Liberty.

Ill. 33

34. Poseidon or Zeus from Histiaea, attributed to the sculptor, Calamis. Heroic size (i.e. between six and twenty feet in height). Colossal statues are those more than twenty feet high.

35. Perhaps the best known of all surviving Greek bronzes, the *Charioteer of Delphi*, about 470 BC. This once formed part of a group commemorating a chariot victory.

The old tradition, if unlikely, is not impossible however. A very large Buddhist figure, sixty-five feet in height, was cast in Japan in the early years of the seventeenth century of our era in this way, the metal being poured into moulds continually added as each section was finished. Many difficulties were encountered, however, and about fifteen per cent of lead was added to the alloy to ensure easy pouring. Aitchison (*A History of Metals*) suggests that the Colossos was built largely of sheet metal and supported by stone pillars and iron scaffolding, but this is conjectural and without confirmation.

Whatever the method employed the Colossos was no isolated phenomenon. Strabo refers to a statue by Phidias of Athene Promachos which was fifty feet in height, erected as a guide to mariners, and the Colossos itself, overthrown in an earthquake, fathered a whole series of giant statues, of which the most comparable in size was one of Nero in Rome, 110 feet in height, which gave its name to the Colosseum when this was built nearby. This, the work of Zenodorus, was later removed by Hadrian with the assistance of twenty-four elephants. Also in Rome was the Apollo in the Capitol, brought from Apollonia, which was about forty-five feet high; the Tuscan Apollo on the Palatine Hill was fifty feet in height and greatly admired for its workmanship, and the armour of the conquered Samnites was melted to make an immense statue of Jupiter Latiaris on the Alban Mount.

Vast quantities of Near and Middle Eastern merchandise began to arrive in Greece soon after 800 BC, brought by Greek and Phoenician traders and seamen, and before 700 BC Greek art had entered what is often termed its 'Orientalizing' phase, when Egyptian and Assyrian *motifs* exerted extensive influence. Native craftsmen of both Greece and Italy reproduced Eastern ornament so closely that the true origin of some objects is even in doubt.

Cauldrons on a tripod stand with, in the case of the earliest examples, animal heads round the rim, are followed by those with human figures on the vessel rims, and sometimes handles in the form of animals. Some of the early figures to be seen today as isolated bronzes originally formed part of a vessel such as this. One especially

36. Griffin's head from a cauldron. Greek. 630 BC. The griffin, with the body of a lion and the head and wings of an eagle, came from Mesopotamian sources.

fine specimen has figures of Scythian horsemen round the rim, and it is worthy of note that vessels with figures similarly disposed occur about the same date in China.

Small reliefs ornamented with figures, heraldic animals, and so forth, surrounded by a formal border, occur during the sixth century. These seem to have been furniture-mounts and they include both strips and corner-pieces. Architectural bronzework has long since disappeared, although Homer testifies to its existence, referring in the *Odyssey* to the palace of Phaeacia's mighty King with 'walls plated bright with brass', and to the palace of Menelaus – 'see what a blaze of copper and gold and electrum and silver and ivory goes through this echoing hall'.

The sixth century BC – the beginning of the Classical period – was perhaps the period of the finest statuettes, and they were now made in much greater quantities. Not only were they offered, in the form

37. Bronze head of Hypnus, god of sleep. Either late fourth century Greek or a Roman copy. Much Greek sculpture has descended to us by way of copies of popular works made in Rome, especially in the first century AD.

of representations of the gods, at various shrines, but it became the custom to journey to Olympia for the Games, and here statuettes were sold by itinerant vendors. Before the end of the pre-Christian era production of statuettes had been organized almost on factory lines, and, like the makers of pottery figures at Tanagra and Myrina, methods of duplicating casts with interchangeable moulds had been devised. It was, however, left to the Romans to commercialize the industry on a large scale, especially at Capua, where the first trade-mark appears to have been used in the first century AD. As well as small statuettes, larger statues of the gods were reproduced for wealthy Greek and Roman tourists, and portraits of well known poets and philosophers were offered for sale.

38. Fountains both public and private were very numerous in ancient Rome, fed by the many aqueducts which brought water to the city from the surrounding hills. Small private fountains at Pompeii, usually set in a niche, were profusely ornamented. Bronze played a large part in the decoration of fountains. This spout is Roman, of the first century AD.

Statuettes and statues of the Archaic period have an inflexibility of pose, the legs straight and the arms at the sides, but a little before 450 BC a new style began to emerge tentatively with a turn of the head or a shifting of the weight from one foot to the other. The effect of these trifling alterations was to impart new life to the figures, and this inspired the modellers to experiment with even more pronounced movement, especially to be seen in statuettes of athletes. The new movement was in full swing by about 450 BC, and, at the same time, the bronzeworker increasingly concerned himself with the rendering of fine detail by chiselling and engraving, finishing the hair with a drill. The eyes were usually inlaid.

Although hollow casting was now well established for large work, hollow-cast statuettes were still extremely rare, but when statuettes began to be collected by wealthy connoisseurs the care lavished on their manufacture became noticeably greater. Personal wealth was increasing rapidly in Rome, which was no longer a community of peasant farmers, and a taste for Greek art developed after the capture of Corinth by Lucius Mummius in 146 BC. Human figures, instead of those of the gods, became the fashion, and dancing attitudes, crouching poses, and well-observed reclining figures relaxed in sleep occur. Representations of foreign warriors – Gauls, Dacians, and Persians – were not unusual subjects, and small children and babies, realistically depicted old age, and even deformities, all came from the modellers of the Greek world. The stylization of the early period gave place to realism, and sometimes to sentimentality. This, the Hellenistic phase, perhaps emanated from Alexandria where there was a large Greek colony, as much as from any single place.

The softness and sensuality of Greek bronzework which begins to be noticeable in the fourth century BC was the product of Persian influence, and although both Scopas (fl. 395–350 BC) and Praxiteles (fl. 240–330 BC) worked largely in marble, they profoundly influenced contemporary bronzes. Praxiteles was attracted to the female form, which had not hitherto enjoyed much popularity among Greek sculptors. A bronze Aphrodite was regarded as equal to his marble Aphrodite at Cnidus, and Pliny considered a bronze courtesan to be a portrait of Phryne, who may also have been the model for the Cnidian statue.

Many experiments were made with alloys to colour the surface of bronzes. The extent to which this was done, and the lengths to which the practice was carried, can now only be guessed. Pliny says that Aristonidas made a statue of Athamas in which he attempted to bring a blush to the face by alloying the bronze with iron. Quite obviously he did not succeed. Plutarch mentions a statue of the dying Jocasta in which silver was included to simulate her pallid complexion. Praxiteles was reputed to have employed an alloy almost of flesh-colour to make a figure of Cupid, but with what success we do not know since Nero removed it to Rome and it perished in the fire of AD 64.

The gilding of bronze was very commonly practised, especially in Rome, and traces of gold sometimes appear on small Roman bronzes. It is probable that whenever ancient writers refer to 'golden' statues gilt-bronze is to be understood if manufacture from gold plates can be excluded.

39. Cast bronze of Aphrodite tying her hair with ribbons. From the Peloponnese. 300–200 BC.

Cast bronze sculpture in both Greece and Rome in Classical times differed from marble in its treatment of subject. The reasons are principally technical, and a general discussion of them is appropriate at this point. The bronzeworker enjoys a freedom denied to the marble-carver because of differences in the structure and properties of the two substances. Marble is brittle. It can resist compressive stresses far more easily than tensile, which accounts for the comparatively short distances separating the pillars supporting the pediment in Classical building. If an arm be outflung from a marble statue at a right-angle to the body the weight imposes a compressive stress at the shoulder, under the armpit, but the upper surface of the arm, where it joins the shoulder, is subjected to a tensile stress which tends to pull the material apart. The weight of the arm needs a very small addition, especially if pressure is applied to the hand, to snap it off. In general, therefore, marble statues avoid free-floating parts (i.e. parts attached to one end only). A marble torso could be posed on relatively fragile legs, but it would be unwise. If, for instance, in the course of removal it were tilted sideways without

40. An Etruscan *biga* or two-horse chariot. This is the older form of chariot. It was no doubt intended for circus use, or for processions and triumphs. The *quadriga* was pulled by four horses, and the use of six or even ten is recorded, some no doubt trace-horses.

being adequately supported, the stress on the legs would no longer be compressive but tensile, and it would break off at the ankles, the weakest point. For this reason outflung arms and statues posed only on legs are not seen in marble. Legs were often covered with drapery from the waist downwards, or, if this was not possible, the statue was given the additional support of a tree-trunk, or a pedestal to one side. Occasional poses were attempted in marble which properly belong to bronze, with additional supports arranged to strengthen dangerous parts, but these look absurd, and they suggest the copying in marble of a pre-existing bronze work.

All these difficulties disappear in the case of bronze. Bronze has a great deal of tensile strength, although not as much as iron or steel, and where tensile stresses are likely to be excessive the metal can easily be thickened internally to take care of them. In the case of an outflung arm the metal should, ideally, be thicker immediately under the top of the shoulder than in the armpit, and other similar instances will readily present themselves. This is not difficult when the lost wax method of casting is being employed, because the wax merely has to be thickened in the appropriate places. As an instance of what is possible we have only to remember the *Mercury* of Giovanni da Bologna, or the *Perseus* of Cellini, the outflung arm of which ends in the head of Medusa.

Ill. 151
Ill. 142

A bronze statue is a cast of a model in some other material, usually clay. Models of clay can be supported internally by armatures of iron rod, and this allows free-floating parts to be modelled without risk of breakage. Of course these add to the difficulty of casting, and they are sometimes made separately and affixed afterwards, but in general the possibilities are almost limitless. Had bronze sculpture survived in greater quantity it would no doubt have been possible to see that well-marked differences in style always existed between works in bronze and in marble, although bronze imitations of admired works in marble, and vice versa, exist. Generally the advantage of bronze is that it imposes few serious limitations on what can be made in it; its disadvantage is that the sculptor cannot work directly, but must hand his model on to someone else for finishing.

41. The *Chimera* of Arezzo. Etruscan. Fourth century BC. Found at Arezzo in 1554, it seems undoubtedly Etruscan, although a Greek origin was claimed for it in the past.

We do not know where the Etruscans came from, and their language is, up till now, largely indecipherable (although some of the words can be read by analogy), but they were highly skilled metalworkers. They were also shrewd sea-traders, exchanging metals for other manufactures and luxuries, and a very large number of bronze objects made by them have been recovered. Pliny pays tribute to their skill in making both large and small bronzes, from *lares* or household gods to colossal statues, such as that of Apollo on the Palatine Hill. Etruscan vessels of bronze were much esteemed, even by the Greeks, and they were extremely skilful engravers.

Generally the art of the Etruscans after *c.* 700 BC falls into two phases. The first is an 'Orientalizing' phase lasting until *c.* 625 BC which more or less corresponds to the same phase in Greek art.

After 625 BC we find a progressive adoption of the new Greek styles which predominated by the fourth century. The Etruscans preferred bronze and terracotta to marble, and they were noted for the fine quality of their tripods (stands for large cauldrons), for engraved caskets, and for vessels of one kind or another. Bronze death-masks were customary, and the portrait bust, popular in Rome by the first century BC, may also have been an attempt to immortalize the subject. Bronze furniture has survived, and armour and weapons of all kinds are well known, shields usually being decorated with embossed work. Some very unusual votive figures of the third century BC have a flat, elongated body and a head modelled in the round. From them the Romans acquired much of their skill as architects and engineers, and three especially fine examples of Etruscan workmanship are shown here. The splendid *Chimera* of the fourth century is now in Florence, the Capitoline She-wolf, of the sixth century,

Ill. 41
Ill. 42

42. The *Capitoline Wolf.* Sixth century BC. Etruscan. The present twins are thought to be a Renaissance addition, perhaps by Giacomo della Porta or Pollaiuolo. Romulus and Remus occur on some ancient medals; on others they are absent. There is some evidence that the twins formed part of the group at the beginning of the present era but may have subsequently disappeared.

is in the Museo dei Conservatore in Rome, and the later *Orator*
Ill. 43 (Aulus Metullus) belongs to the first century BC.

Perhaps the greatest contribution of the Romans to the art of metalwork was in improvements to existing methods of joining metals one to the other, and in creating factory systems for the production of useful works and those of a minor ornamental character. No doubt military necessity played a large part in these developments. When armies were small, and only officers were completely armed and armoured, individual craftsmen could afford to lavish time on the making of pieces which went to make up a complete equipment, but the arming of the Legions was a very different problem, in which each man was given standard equipment that had been developed and tested in service, and this had to be manufactured in large quantities.

The Romans met and overcame this serious problem in logistics. They made far greater use of prefabricated parts in assembling bronze objects of all kinds than had been done hitherto, and for this purpose they developed methods of soldering, welding, brazing, and riveting bronze, as well as techniques of joining differing metals. They were well acquainted with hard and soft soldering, using soldering-irons, blow-pipes for brazing, and resin fluxes. These techniques, however, are not only to be seen in the manufacture of arms, but also that of bronze utensils, plain and decorative, which furnished the Roman home. It is diverting to speculate how much earlier the Industrial Revolution might have occurred in Europe had events permitted Roman manufacturing techniques to reach their logical conclusion.

Statues which, from style and subject, can be regarded as Roman do not begin to appear much before the first century AD. By Imperial times artists resorted to Rome from all parts of the Empire, although most came from Greece, and the art of bronze owed its encouragement principally to the patronage of the great and the

43. The *Orator*. Etruscan. First century BC. In this remarkable full-length statue we can see the origin of a great deal of later Roman portrait sculpture.

wealthy. They bought ornamental metalwork from the many art- and antique-dealers who established themselves in Rome, and there was always a keen demand for works intended to commemorate persons and events, especially statues of the gods to be erected in temples and public places. Pliny, towards the end of his *Natural History*, brings together many references to works which have not survived. Under the heading of 'The Immoderate Price of Statues' he refers to the enormous quantity of bronze statuary existing in the world of his day. But despite the immense number brought to Rome by conquering generals, returning provincial governors, and art-dealers, immense quantities survived outside Rome. There were three thousand in Rhodes, and, Pliny supposed, as many at least in Athens, Olympia, and Delphi. 'What living mortal,' he asks, 'could enumerate them all? And of what use could be such information?' He credits Lysippus alone with fifteen hundred statues, and it is perhaps a comment on the most admired style that a bronze figure of a dog licking its wounds was regarded as so true to life that no sum was thought of as equalling it in value. The keepers of the shrine in which it was housed were held answerable for its safety with their lives.

Ill. 44 The only specimen of large Roman bronze sculpture to survive the vicissitudes of time is the equestrian statue of Marcus Aurelius, now in the Piazza del Campidoglio in Rome, about seventeen feet in height. It was first erected in AD 173, possibly on top of an arch, and it probably owes its survival to the fact that it was thought for many years to represent the Christian Emperor Constantine. It is undoubted that many such equestrian statues existed in Rome in the first centuries of the present era, and this particular survival fathered a whole series of later equestrian bronze statues which will be considered in their place. Equestrian statues were always much esteemed in the classical world, especially in Rome. The Greeks commonly commemorated victors in the sacred games in this way, particularly those who had gained the palm in chariot-races.

Pliny records that naked statues brandishing spears were much admired, and were called 'Achillean'. A familiar modern example is the memorial to the Duke of Wellington by Westmacott in Hyde

44. The equestrian Marcus Aurelius in the Piazza del Campidoglio, Rome, originally may have had a man under the horse's hoof. In former times it was regarded as representing both Constantine and Septimus Severus. It has been repaired on several occasions, notably by Sixtus IV who paid substantial sums to Roman goldsmiths in 1473, and in 1836 by Thorwaldsen. It was removed from the Lateran to the present site in 1538.

Park, near Apsley House. The Greek practice was to make such statues entirely nude, but the Romans came to give their athletes and military figures the cuirass and light armour. Many statues were erected in honour of popular heroes, such as one to Horatius Cocles, the 'one-eyed' who defended the Sublician Bridge against Lars Porsena and the Etruscan army, which was still to be seen in Pliny's day. There is even record of one named, appropriately enough, Spurius Cassius, who erected a statue to himself, but the Censors ordered it to be taken down and melted lest he become too ambitious.

The view that Roman sculpture is merely an inferior variant of Greek is too harsh. Portraiture owes little to Greek influence, and it is a generalization worth making that drapery is a special characteristic of Roman work. A writer of the Renaissance reproached the Romans for having no word for symmetry, and it is true that they took little interest in the strict canons of sculptural proportion and

45. Mounted warrior, probably intended for Alexander the Great and taken from a group dedicated by Alexander to commemorate the defeat of the Persians in the Battle of Granicus, 334 BC. Roman. Imperial period.

measurement laid down by the Greeks. Perhaps the most notable difference between Roman portrait sculpture and that of Greece is that the former is essentially a statement about a particular human being, whereas the latter is about human beings in general. Collections, both public and private, were filled with Greek work however, and it is essential to remember that neither the Romans nor the Greeks distinguished between craftsmen and that scarcely definable invention of nineteenth- and twentieth-century art-criticism, the genius, whose destiny it is to express his ego. The sculptor took his customer's order for a particular subject intended for a designated place and purpose.

Carried in the funeral procession of the patrician Roman were the death-masks of his ancestors, a custom taken from the Etruscans. This led to a demand for realistic portraits made during the lifetime of the person represented. From the first century BC Rome offered the portrait sculptor the chance of a lucrative career, and bronze was a favoured material for portraits. At first little more than the head and neck, the area was gradually increased until the first century AD the whole of the shoulders and most part of the chest had been taken in. That they are good likenesses is evident because idiosyncracies of feature and expression are nearly always well marked. Portrait heads of the Emperors are relatively frequent survivals because many were made to be sent to the seats of provincial government, for much the same reason as every German Embassy before the war had its bust of Adolf Hitler.

Statues of the Emperors are usually posed in an oratorical attitude customary when addressing the Legions, something to which particular importance was attached, as witness the many such orations preserved by Roman historians. Oratory was a cultivated art, to which the illustrated statue of the Orator testifies. A lifelike appearance was often attained by inlaying the eyes, and surviving busts with a circular scoop of metal representing the iris may or may not have been thus treated. Unlike the Greeks, the Romans had no compunction in depicting baldness wherever appropriate.

Greek influence was especially strong during the reign of Hadrian, a noted patron of the arts who had a reputation as a sculptor, although nothing has been attributed to his hand. Spartianus says that Hadrian's talents almost equalled those of Polycletes. The Greek style was again favoured by Antinous and Alexander Severus, the latter being a noted connoisseur of bronze statuary in his day.

Generally, the Greeks were disinclined to sell antique works of art, and despite the large quantities of statues carried off by Mummius, Fulvus Nobilior, and Verres, there is no doubt that by far the greater number remained in Greece. Nero ordered extensive depredations in Greece and the Greek colonies of Asia Minor to replace work destroyed during the great fire of AD 64. Five hundred bronzes were removed from Delphi, and a like number from Olympia. The

46. The bronze horses of St Mark's, Venice. These exerted almost as much influence on Renaissance equestrian sculpture as the *Marcus Aurelius (Ill. 44)*. Of uncertain origin, they are thought to have been brought to Rome by Augustus, and removed to Byzantium by Constantine, who set them up in the Hippodrome.

47. Bronze horse excavated at Herculaneum. *Cf. Ill. 46.*

Etruscans were even greater sufferers, and according to Pliny two thousand bronzes were brought to Rome from one Etruscan city. It is some indication of the number existing in Greece that Pausanias in his later travels saw little to suggest extensive plundering.

Much greater damage was done by Christian hostility to ancient works of art. Many bronze statues of the former gods were melted during the reign of Constantine, and the Pantheon was stripped of its roofing. Under Theodosius this vandalism spread to other parts of the Empire, and many Greek bronzes were melted to make a colossal statue of the Byzantine Emperor Anastasius *c.* 500. Even then much remained, but more were melted to cast the Emperor Heraclius a century or so later (see p. 82). The rest were consigned to the melting-pot by the Crusaders in 1204. These brigands revealed a remarkable talent for destruction, bronzes being smashed and piled in the churches for melting. Almost the sole survivors seem to have been the four horses of St Mark's. These, weighing about two tons apiece with a height of almost six feet, are sometimes thought to be the work of Lysippus of Chios, but it seems more likely that they were once part of a triumphal arch, drawing a car

Ill. 46

driven by Victory and cast in honour of Nero. Constantine removed them to the new capital of the Empire to adorn the Imperial hippodrome. In 1797 they were looted by Napoleon to surmount the Triumphal Arch in the Place du Carrousel, and they were returned to Venice in 1814 after the intervention of Francis I of Austria. According to the historian Sanudo, who published the Venetian State Papers, the hind hoof of one of them was broken off in transit to Venice in 1204 and begged as a souvenir by the master of the galley which brought them. It was given to him, and the broken hoof restored with new metal.

Of all the bronzes which existed in Pliny's day, good and bad, nothing, apart from Marcus Aurelius, the Venice horses, and some architectural metalwork, were to be found above ground. The survivors have been excavated.

Most prized among the smaller excavated works in bronze are figures, many of nondescript quality but a few extremely fine. Some of these relate to the cult of the Lares Familiaris – images worshipped in an inner part of the house called the 'Lararium'. The custom, revived by Augustus, continued at least until the time of Alexander Severus who is reputed to have had in his principal

48. Bucket (*situla*). At the bottom a representation of Hercules struggling with the Nemean Lion. Handles in the form of harpies snatching two boys. Etruscan. 400–300 B C.

49. Bronze mirrors, often finely engraved on the reverse, are among the best surviving examples of this kind of decoration. The subject here is Aphrodite and Pan gaming. Greek. Fourth century BC. Long mirrors attached to a wall existed, but have not survived.

Lararium images of Christ, Orpheus, Abraham, and Alexander the Great – an eclectic taste. Bronze figures of gladiators were made for a different purpose, and some are remarkable for the care and skill which were lavished on them. Gladiators first appeared in Rome in 264 BC, and the combats soon became extremely popular, being the subject of large wagers and fierce partisanship. These figures are usually realistically modelled, their angular poses lending them an air of ferocity. The finest ornamental figures were so highly regarded that their owners often carried them about.

50. Although glass mirrors may have existed in the first century AD in Rome, they never came into general use. The vast majority of ancient Greek and Roman mirrors were of polished bronze. This example, among the earliest, comes from Greece, made about 450 BC.

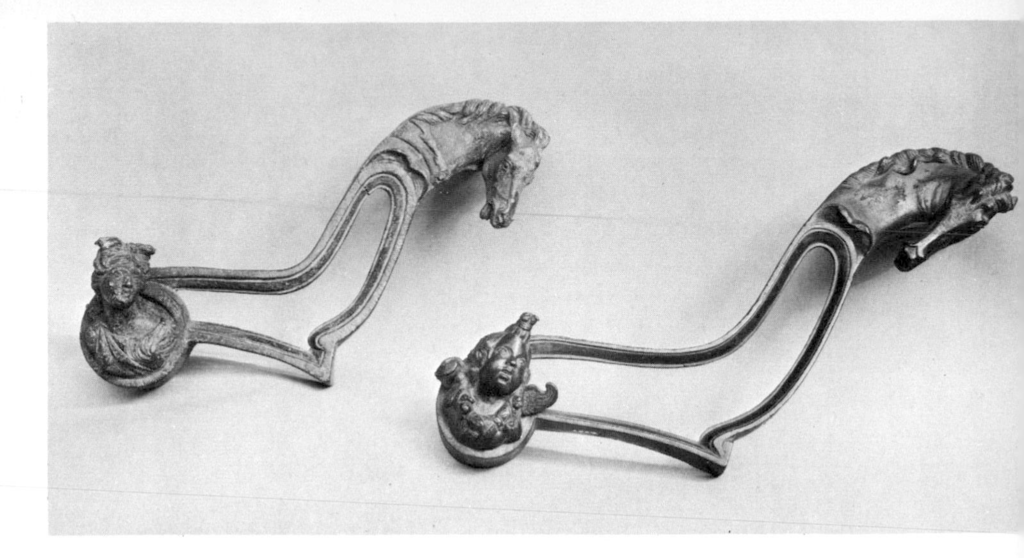

51. A pair of end-supports for a couch, once in the collection of Sir William Hamilton. Probably from Herculaneum or Pompeii. First century AD. The mounting of furniture in this way was already ancient in Roman times and it formed an essential part of French furniture design in the seventeenth and eighteenth centuries.

There is insufficient space to mention the many bronze vessels, but among the finest was the *patera*, a circular dish which was often handsomely decorated. The *krater* was a large vessel in which wine was mixed with water by ancient custom. According to Herodotus the Lacedaemonians sent as a gift to Croesus, King of Lydia, a brazen *krater* so large that it could hold the contents of three hundred *amphorae*, the Greek measure known as the *amphoreus* being equivalent to about eight gallons. *Situlae* were buckets or pails, the finest of which were handsomely decorated. The *pyxis* was a jewel casket, the best finely ornamented with embossed and chiselled work and engraving. Mirrors were frequently decorated with linear engraving. The best bronze mirrors (says Pliny) were made in Brundisium before everyone, even the maid-servants, took to using mirrors of silver. Those of bronze needed frequent repolishing, and a sponge and powdered pumice were often attached to them for the purpose. In Greece exceptionally handsome mirrors date back to the sixth century BC. Handle and mirror were made separately,

Ill. 48

Ills. 49, 50

probably because mirror-bronze was an alloy containing a much greater amount of tin than it was customary to use for other work.

Bronze was extensively used in the decoration of furniture, and the principal source of these mounts was probably Capua where vast quantities of ordinary domestic bronzeware were made. Lighting appliances of all kinds were usually of bronze, terracotta being employed only for the cheapest lamps. Etruscan candelabra are finely decorated, although Roman candelabra, made in much greater numbers, are plainer because of the need to manufacture them in easily assembled parts.

Ill. 51

Apart from mass-produced weapons for the Legions, Greek and Roman armour can often be regarded as a work of art. Shields were sometimes profusely ornamented, although these were parade shields and not intended for serious use. Body-armour was carefully tailored to individual requirements, and Xenophon (*Memorabilia of Socrates*) recounts at length a discussion which accompanied a visit to the armourer for a fitting, and sets out the features to be desired in a well-tailored cuirass. Homer's heroes were, according to his

52. Greek cuirass of the fourth century BC.

53. A very rare gladiator's parade helmet with a head of Hercules above the visor. Second century A D. Helmets of this kind were worn in conjunction with richly decorated armour and weapons, especially in the preliminary ceremonial parade round the amphitheatre.

descriptions, walking colossi of bronze, but from Plutarch we cull some information about the actual weight of body-armour. A light outfit might tip the scale at about thirty pounds, and a whole suit of unusual weight at about a hundredweight. The cuirass was shaped to the prominences and hollows of the body by hammering, suspended from the shoulders by leather straps, and fastened at the sides with buckles. A Greek helmet is shown here, and a much more elaborate Roman gladiator's helmet, which the maker has taken pains to decorate. The latter is not solely a parade helmet, but it was not intended for the rigours of general battle.

Ill. 52
Ill. 54
Ill. 53

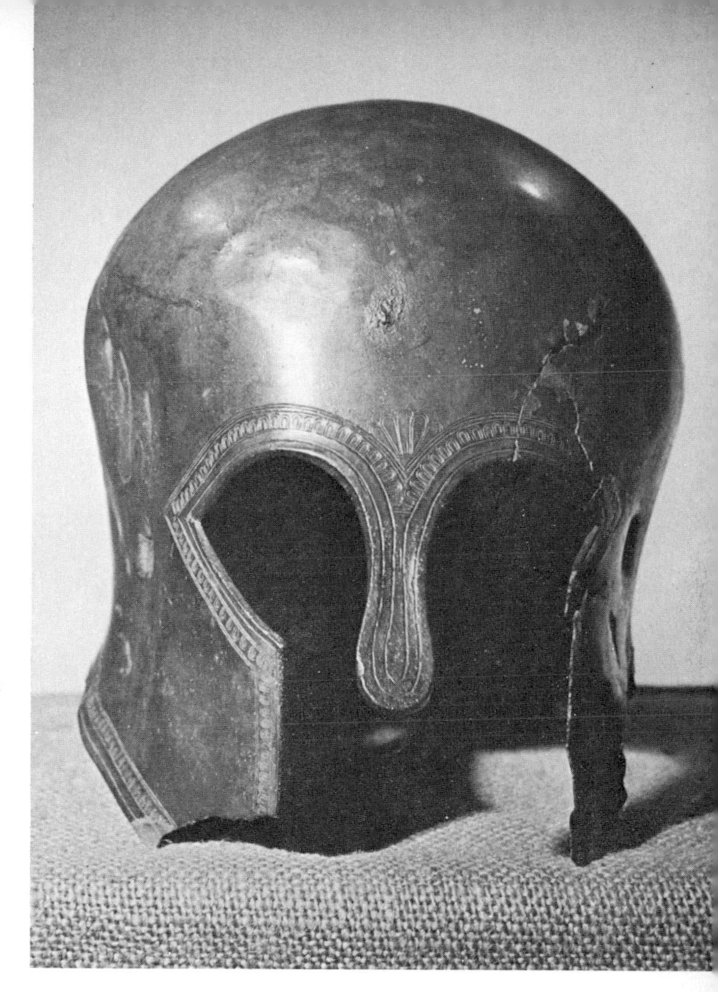

54. Greek helmet of the fifth century BC in an excellent state of preservation. The attachment for the crest has almost disappeared but its position can still be seen.

The Romans in particular were connoisseurs of bronze. Corinthian bronze (*aes Corinthiacum*) was more highly valued than silver. Its origin was thought to be the burning of Corinth in 146 BC, when Mummius exacted revenge for an outburst of exuberance on the part of the populace, who emptied their chamber-pots over the heads of Roman ambassadors. It was believed that vessels of bronze, gold, and silver, melted by the heat had run together to form a new alloy. Pliny mentions three kinds of Corinthian bronze – *candidum*, which was light in colour and thought to contain silver; a marked golden colour which he believed to be due to the addition of gold;

and a third variety composed of an equal amount of the various metals. This, however, can be no more than market-place gossip, probably put about by dealers of the day, and analyses have not borne out Pliny's suppositions. It is extremely doubtful whether gold was ever used as an alloying metal in Classical bronzes, and we may seek for the cause of the belief in the word *aurichalcum* (often spelled *orichalcum*) used for one kind of bronze. This was taken to refer to gold, but the origin is actually in the Greek *oros*, a mountain, and *chalkos*, metal – mountain metal, a reference to the source of the ore. Pliny's golden bronze is much more likely to have been brass. *Hepatizon* was, as the name suggests, a liver-coloured bronze, and it had its origin in Delos and the Aegina. *Aes Deliacum*, named after the island of Delos, which was a notable metalworking centre, was

55 (*left*). *Autumn* (Pomona). Imperial Roman period. She is reminiscent in style of some late seventeenth-century French *bronzes d'ameublement*.

56 (*right*). A Roman bronze figure of Pan. First century AD. *Cf.* the satyr from Riccio's workshop, *Ill. 137*.

probably next in order of popularity. It was seemingly light in colour. *Aes Aegineticum* came from Aegina, where the bronzesmiths were also celebrated. Philostratus mentions *aes nigrum*, which was probably black or near-black.

Inlaying, and covering bronze with silver and gold, leads to an even greater degree of corrosion than is usual if an object has been buried. For this reason gilded bronzes are rare, although traces of gilding can sometimes be identified. Mercuric gilding was well known to the Romans, and they used mercury for refining gold. Leaf-gold seems to have been used occasionally, although the relevant passage in the *Natural History* is obscure. Certainly leaf-gold was well known to the Romans. Tinning was a common way of making copper vessels fit for containing food. Pliny says that when tinned 'they produce a less disagreeable flavour, and the formation of verdigris is prevented'.

The process of tinning copper vessels has hardly been improved since Pliny's day. By mixing equal parts of lead and tin a pewter was produced called *argentarium*, which was also sometimes used fraudulently to simulate silver. *Tertiarium* was two parts of lead to one of tin – the equivalent of common solder – which was principally employed for joining pipes. Its price was twenty denarii a pound. A confusion between lead and tin undoubtedly contributed to the prevalence of lead-poisoning in Rome.

Little is known of the methods employed for casting statues and portrait busts. Both clay and gypsum were used to make original models, but it would be hazardous to go on from this and assume that gypsum plaster was used for moulding also. Pliny appears to say in the *Natural History* (XXXIV.xii) that Lysistratus, brother of Lysippus, used plaster to take casts from life in the fourth century BC. If this is correct, and there is no reason why it should not be, then plaster was certainly used to take moulds from clay originals. To make moulds suitable for bronze-casting from plaster, however, means that some refractory material must be added, and its use for this purpose remains unproven. No doubt moulds made from refractory clay were commonly used for bronze-casting, and the lost wax technique was employed wherever appropriate.

This chapter would not be complete without mention of various automatic and mechanical devices made in ancient Rome. Such devices as those of Hero for opening temple doors automatically when fire was lit on a distant altar required a good deal of bronze-work made to fairly fine limits of tolerance, but perhaps the best evidence of Roman ingenuity is to be seen in the remains of a double-acting water-pump with flap valves.

Ill. 57

With the fall of the Empire bronze lost much of its importance, and although a certain amount of fine work was done between then and the beginning of the Renaissance, the metal never regained its former importance in the manufacture of objects of utility.

57. Roman technical achievements can only be guessed from such survivals as the fragmentary works of the engineer Hero of Alexandria (*c.* 100 BC) which include a description of a double-acting pump for a fire-engine. This shows a very rare survival of a Roman pump.

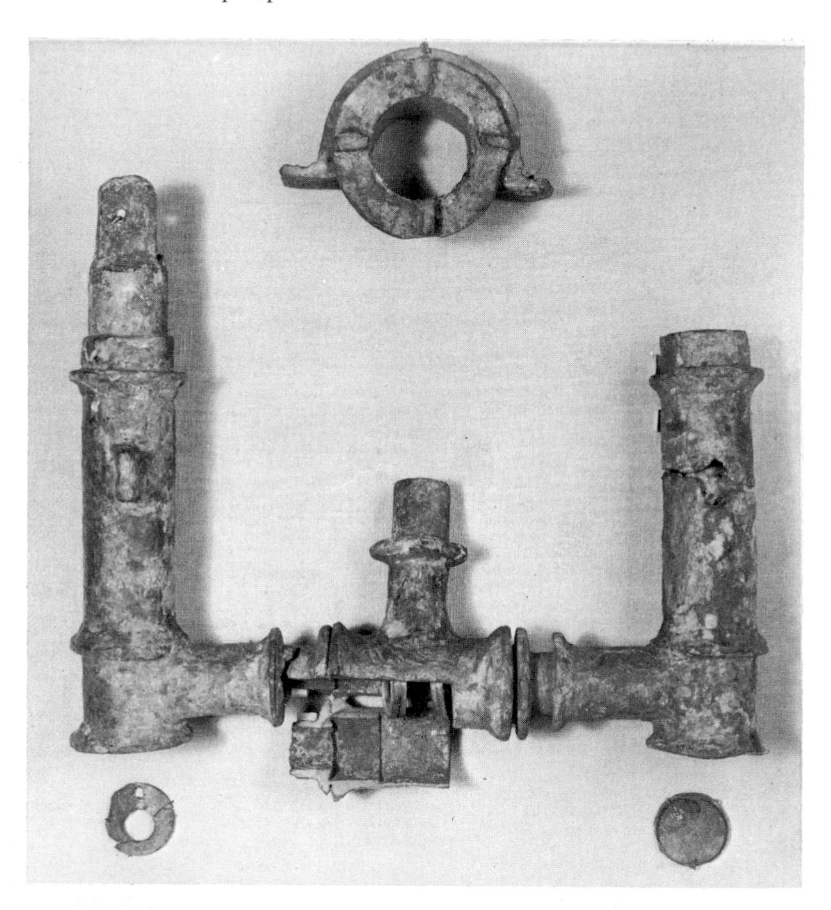

CHAPTER THREE

Romanesque and Gothic bronzework

Between the fall of the Western Roman Empire, which followed the sack of the Eternal City by the barbarians in 455, and the post-Carolingian phase, known as 'Romanesque', which began early in the tenth century numerous incursions by nomads from the east completed what the incompetence of later Roman rule had started. These nomads followed a route which traversed the northern frontiers of the Eastern Roman Empire, of which Byzantium was the capital, into the south Russian plains, and ultimately a great deal of northern Europe fell to them.

Earlier invaders, such as the Goths and the Vandals, were pushed westwards, to the south and the north, by the Hsiung-nu, Mongol Huns from territory to the north of China, whose European empire at its furthest extent penned the indigenous tribes against the North Sea. A good deal of Hun territory was later occupied by the Avars (the White Huns), and by the Turkish Khazans. These invasions, and the irruptions of the armies of Islam into the Near and Middle East, brought new influences to the West, although they are not always especially obvious. Both nomadic and Middle Eastern art influenced that of northern Europe especially, although the old Classical traditions, modified by circumstances, were stronger and much more persistent in the countries bordering the Mediterranean.

During this period sculpture in bronze largely gave way to that in stone and other materials, and for a long period metalwork generally was principally confined to bronze doors, tombs, and ecclesiastical vessels. The use of the precious metals, common in Byzantium, was replaced further west by copper and bronze, often gilded and sometimes enamelled.

The tradition of bronze sculpture survived in Byzantium, although we can only guess to what extent. During the reign of Justinian (483–565) a pillar sheathed with bronze was made and surmounted by an equestrian statue of the Emperor which was thirty feet high. Unlike others, this survived until the sixteenth century. An heroic bronze statue, probably of the Emperor Heraclius (610–41), and thought to be the work of a Greek named Polyphobus, was washed ashore on the Apulian coast like a stranded whale, to be salvaged by the inhabitants of Barletta. It was part of the loot of Byzantium in 1204, and seems to have been one of the bronzes (which included the horses of St Mark's) that were shipped to Venice at this time. The Emperor remained lying at Barletta until 1491, when he was repaired by a bronze-founder, Albanus Fabius from Naples, and set up in the Piazza.

Ill. 58

Bronze doors, such as those which had closed the portals of the Roman Pantheon, had been made for Sancta Sophia in Byzantium in the days of Justinian, and the earliest post-Roman Italian doors were the work of a bronze-founder named Staurachios and cast in Byzantium. These were presented to the Benedictine monastery of Monte Cassino in 1087 by the Pantaleone family of Amalfi, who also gave doors to churches in Amalfi, Atrano, and Monte Gargano. It is at this time that we notice the use in Italy of the Byzantine alloy of silver, lead, and sulphur known as 'niello', which first occurs in the ninth century, and for which Theophilus (*De Diversis Artibus*) gives manufacturing directions.

Ill. 59

Staurachios appears to have maintained a workshop for the manufacture of doors, and not surprisingly the design of some Byzantine doors of the period seems to have been based on ivory-carving. That manufacture was well organized is also proved by the occurrence of identical designs in several places, suggesting the use of the same prototypes. Some of the doors of the time are damascened in silver, an Islamic technique.

The doors of San Zeno Maggiore in Verona, made from poor-quality embossed panels riveted to a wooden foundation, were the work of Saxon artificers, but these are relatively late, being installed in the twelfth century. The finest German work certainly antedates

58. Heroic bronze statue thought to be either the Emperor Heraclius or Theodosius. Cast in Byzantium probably in the seventh century AD.

SACRO CUORE DI GESU'
VIVA
IL CUORE DI GESU'
DOLCE CUORE DEL MIO GESU'
SACRO CUORE DI GESU'
VENGA IL TUO REGNO
PER MEZZO DI MARIA
SACRO CUORE DI GESU'
VIVA
IL CUORE DI GESU'
DOLCE CUORE DEL MIO GESU'
SACRO CUORE DI GESU'
VENGA IL TUO REGNO
PER MEZZO DI MARIA

59 (*left*). This bronze door of two sets of eighteen engraved and inlaid panels was made in 1066 for the Monastery of Monte Cassino by Staurachios, and was the gift of the Pantaleone family of Amalfi.

60. The bronze doors of Bishop Bernward at Hildesheim, made in 1015 and installed in 1033. A cast of these, and the *Christussäule* in the same place, is to be seen in the Victoria and Albert Museum, London.

the doors of Staurachios. In the days of Charlemagne (*c.* 742–814) those of the west portal of Aachen Cathedral were locally cast. Dating from 804 they are simple in design, and each has at its centre a lion-mask sanctuary ring. Much, perhaps most, of the metalwork of the time was made by monks, and this was a continuing tradition. At Mainz the bronze doors of the Cathedral were executed by order of Archbishop Willigis in 988, a fact recorded by a Latin inscription on the borders of the valves.

By far the most important ecclesiastical bronzeworker in Germany, however, was Bishop Bernward of Hildesheim, a few miles south of Hanover, who founded a notable school of bronzeworkers, some examples of whose work are illustrated here. A magnificent pair of doors now at the western end of the Cathedral, which has been restored after damage during the last war, were originally intended for the Church of St Michael not far away. They were installed in the Cathedral in 1033, and each valve is 4·71 metres high and 1·12 metres broad, with a weight of two metric tons. Each has eight panels in relief, those of the left depicting the Fall of Man, and those of the right the Birth and Death of Christ. A narrow band on each valve bears an inscription recording that Bernward made them in 1015 to the glory of God and as his own memorial. The one on the left reads ANDOMINC̄M̄XVBEPDIVM̄EM̄HASVALVAS-FVSILES, and on the right, INFACIĒANGELCTĒPLIOB-MONTM̄T̄SVIFFECSVSPENDI. FVSILES at the end of the first line denotes a pouring out, and refers to the act of casting.

Ill. 60

Ill. 61

The depth of the relief-modelling varies, the architectural backgrounds being lightly raised from the surface and some of the details indicated by chiselling. The figures themselves vary from shallow relief to a three-dimensional projection from the surface, the heads emerging completely from the background. These doors, in fact, mark the beginning of a new phase in European art, since they were the first to be decorated with figurative reliefs. The door on the south side of Augsburg Cathedral, also of the eleventh century, is similar in style, although the panels are more numerous, while in the twelfth century a border of arabesques was first added to reliefs, to be found on the doors of the Cathedral of Gnesen in Poland for

61. Panel from one of Bernward's doors depicting the Fall of Man.

example. These were the work of the bronzesmiths of Lower Saxony whose reputation was well established by the twelfth century. Bronze doors, however, belong to the Romanesque period. Gothic doors of the thirteenth century and later were of plain wood decorated by the blacksmith with wrought-iron traceries, although a few carved wood doors survive.

Apart from the doors described other important works in bronze came from Bernward, notable among them the *Christussäule*, or Christ's Column, now in the Cathedral, which was inspired by Trajan's Column. Four metres in height, this column has twenty-eight reliefs of scenes from the Life of Christ winding round it. It was Bernward's last work, executed between 1015 and 1022.

Elsewhere in Hildesheim, among the treasures of the Magdalenenkirche, may be found a pair of candlesticks by Bernward which are still used on the altar. These were cast in four parts – the pricket and drip-pans, the stem in two parts, and the base on which is an inscription in niello. The inscription is at present unreadable but could be made legible by cleaning. Bases of similar form ascribed to

Ill. 62

Ill. 63

62. The Bernward Candlesticks, now in the Magdalenenkirche at Hildesheim, are probably the oldest altar-candlesticks still in regular use. Like the Gloucester Candlestick *(Ill. 64)* they were cast in parts and assembled.

63. The foot of a gilt-bronze cross. German. Hildesheim. Second half of the eleventh century. It is related to the design of the base of pricket candlesticks of the period *(Ills. 62, 64)* which were also intended for the altar.

64. The Gloucester Candlestick. The finest existing example of its kind. Later than the Bernward Candlesticks, it is now considered to be the work of Anglo-Norman craftsmen, although a German origin was at one time suggested for it.

the Bernward school serve equally well for a candlestick or a cross. Later than the Bernward candlesticks, but still belonging to the Romanesque period, is the well known Gloucester candlestick discovered in France and bought by the Victoria and Albert Museum in 1861. The evidence for an English origin for this remarkable candlestick is strong, and it is sometimes described as Anglo-Norman. Like the candlesticks of Bernward it is cast in sections – foot, stem, and drip-pan – the parts being held together by a central iron rod terminating in the pricket. An inscription records that the Abbot Peter and his 'gentle flock' gave it to the Church of St Peter at Gloucester, and another that Thomas of Poche gave it to the Treasury of the Church of Le Mans, an event which seems to have taken place in the thirteenth century.

Ill. 64

Much larger candlesticks than those of Bernward existed during the Romanesque period, often based on the seven-branched candlestick of the Jewish Temple. One at Brunswick, executed for Henry the Lion, is fourteen feet high, comparable with the well known candlestick in Milan Cathedral, the lower part of which is probably of French rather than Italian workmanship. This, however, was originally a single candlestick, the remaining branches being a sixteenth-century addition.

Ills. 65, 66

Some remarkable candlesticks survive from the Gothic period, among the earliest being those resembling the aquamanile in form. Very rare objects of both kinds are attributed to the Meuse school, whence came a good deal of important bronzework in the early years of the Gothic style. Both here, and the Rhineland, were noted both for metalworking and enamelling. In general, however, not a

65, 66. The Milan Candlestick, from Milan Cathedral. Late twelfth century. The origin of this superb work has been much disputed, but an attribution to Nicholas Verdun, a goldsmith of the Mosan school, has much to commend it.

great deal of early French bronzework has survived, principally because Louis Quatorze detested the style and consigned much of it to be melted. Enamelled objects, particularly reliquaries, such as the *chasse*, made at Limoges, are a little more numerous, probably because they belonged to church Treasuries. However, Martin Lister, in Paris in 1698, refers to the scarcity of Limoges enamel at the time, saying it was then hardly to be had.

Relatively the aquamanile is a frequent survival. Most of the larger museums can show at least one specimen. As the name suggests it was made for containing water for the purpose of washing the hands, and it is often in the form of a lion, filled through an opening in the back and pouring from the mouth, the tail curving over to form a handle. It occurs in a variety of forms – for instance, as a medieval mounted knight, or perhaps as an animal based on those to be found in medieval bestiaries. The aquamanile was originally accompanied by a basin (not matching) to contain the water after pouring. The aquamanile in the form of a lion survived in Persia until the seventeenth century.

67 (*far left*). Equestrian aquamanile. English. *c.* 1300. Usually accompanied by a basin (not matching), aquamaniles were used at table to pour scented water over the hands of guests between courses.

68 (*left*). *Simsonleuchter* – a pricket candlestick of brass in the form of Samson astride a lion. North German. Thirteenth century.

69 (*above*). Aquamanile in the form of a centaur. French. Thirteenth century. Vessels of this kind, as often of brass as of bronze, were usually made by the bell-founders.

70 (*right*). Bronze water-jug in the form of a seated lion. North German. Thirteenth century.

71. Head reliquary of gilded bronze. German. Second half of the twelfth century. Caskets such as this, frequently in the form of the part they enclosed, often contained relics of the saints.

In a troubled age monks carried the bones of the saints about with them in cases called reliquaries. These gradually became more elaborate and less portable and were sometimes made in the form of the relic they were intended to contain. A head reliquary is shown here; arm reliquaries were sometimes made with a finger pointing to heaven. When the whole of the skeleton was to be enclosed larger sarcophagi in Romanesque times sometimes took the form of small models of churches, and those of the Gothic period were also treated architecturally, but with the characteristic pointed arches and buttresses of the style, which replaced the Romanesque semicircular arch. Reliquaries were occasionally in the form of the attribute of a particular saint, such as the ship of St Ursula, and all were made in a variety of materials – the finest in the precious metals. Carved and gilded wood, with painted panels, is also to be found in the Gothic period, such as the Shrine of St Ursula of carved and gilded oak with panels by Hans Memling in Bruges, which is reminiscent of contemporary metalwork.

Ill. 71

During the Romanesque and Gothic periods most bronze objects were made for religious purposes. In Italy many were of pure copper, mercurically gilded, and in northern Europe the metal in common use seems to have been a kind of brass rather than true bronze. Theophilus refers to the employment of calamine in alloys of this kind.

Survivals include crosses, pyxes, monstrances (which were sometimes reliquaries), censers, fonts, sanctuary rings, and other kinds of church furniture. Fonts of metal occur more frequently in the Gothic period, although earlier examples still exist. Sometimes of large size, and intended for baptism by immersion, one font at least was partly inspired by Solomon's Brazen Sea – that cast in 1112 by a Dinant craftsman, Lambertus Patras, for St Bartholomew's at Liège, which rests on twelve brazen bulls. Covers of medieval fonts were extremely heavy, and pulleys were sometimes supplied for raising them.

72 Most fonts were of stone, some are of lead, and bronze is relatively scarce. This example from Hildesheim is exceptional. Thirteenth century.

73. Bronze sanctuary-ring or knocker from Durham Cathedral. The lion-mask was used as a handle or knocker during Imperial Roman times.

The sanctuary ring was commonly in the form of a lion-mask with a ring in its mouth, and no doubt it functioned also as a knocker or the handle of a heavy door. Fugitives who could reach and grasp the ring before they were captured enjoyed the protection of the Church.

The censer, or thurible, developed as early as the Romanesque period from a simple form into a vessel with two parts, the upper part in the form of a building, the smoke escaping through window-like openings. The cover was in some cases intended to represent the heavenly city of Jerusalem. Provision was made for the attachment of suspensory chains. Gothic specimens, usually the more elaborate, conform to the prevailing architectural style.

Very little free-standing metal sculpture from this period has survived, and little was made. An example from the Romanesque period is shown, while to the Gothic period belongs the *Schalmeiblasender* (or piper), cast in 1380 and apparently unique. It once formed part of the fountain of the Heilig-Geist-Spital in Nürnberg, and originally spouted water from the pipe and ears. Cast by the lost wax method, it is a copy of a carved wood prototype, this being a favourite medium in the city which was the home of Veit Stoss. Another bronze fountain, the *Gänsemännchen* at Nürnberg, later described, actually exists in both the wooden and bronze versions.

Ill. 76
Ill. 77

74 The bronze thurible of Godric. English. Tenth or eleventh century. Thuribles, usually of bronze, were incense-burners, as the pierced top shows. Incense was first used in Christian churches in the sixth century.

75. Mask of a youth crowned with a wreath. From a Nürnberg fountain. End of the fifteenth century.

76. *Madonna*. Gilded bronze. German. Twelfth century. Probably a late work from the school founded at Hildesheim by Bernward. Surviving metal sculpture from this period is exceedingly rare.

77. The *Schalmeibläsender* Hansel, a player on a shawm which was a kind of pipe. From a Nürnberg fountain. *c.* 1380. This is a rare and lively example of Gothic sculpture in bronze.

Elsewhere metal sculpture is usually to be found decorating tombs. The oldest surviving bronze of this kind, a relief of Rudolf of Swabia in Merseburg Castle, was executed at the end of the eleventh century, but most such tombs are Gothic in style. In England, of a series of early royal effigies, we may select Henry III (d. 1272) in Westminster Abbey, which was the work of a London goldsmith, William Torrell, perhaps originally Torelli of Italian origin. For the effigy of Queen Eleanor, completed in 1392, a record exists of the delivery of wax to the founder.

Ill. 78

For the making of the tomb of the Black Prince in Canterbury Cathedral, which may have been the work of John Orchard although it is sometimes attributed to craftsmen from Limoges, detailed instructions survive in the Prince's will. 'The tomb shall be made of marble . . . and above the tomb shall be made a table of laton [brass] over gilt . . . upon which we will that an image in relieved work of laton gilt shall be placed in memory of us, all armed in steel for

78. Recumbent figure of the Black Prince from his tomb in Canterbury Cathedral. Fourteenth century. The face is undoubtedly a portrait in which it is possible to trace the Plantagenet features. The sword, now missing, is said to have been removed by Cromwell.

79. Altar-tomb of the Earl of Warwick, Beauchamp Chapel, Warwick Castle. William Austen, the founder, and Thomas Stevyns, coppersmith, were engaged on 13 June 1453 'to cast and make the image of a man armed' and 'fourteen embossed images of lords and ladies' of 'the finest latten'.

80. Bronze bowl engraved with the figure of Cadmus and the Labours of Hercules. English. Twelfth century. Cadmus was reputed to be the discoverer of many of the useful arts.

81 *(right)*. Dish with embossed decoration from Dinant, or perhaps from near-by Malines. The subject is a common one in the medieval period – the pelican feeding her young with drops of blood pecked from her breast. *c.* 1480. Work of this kind from Dinant is often called *dinanderie*.

battle, with our arms quartered; and my visage with our helmet of the leopard put under the head of the image. . . .'

Ill. 79 Of considerable interest are the surviving accounts for the monument to Richard Beauchamp, Earl of Warwick, which is in the Beauchamp Chapel of St Mary's Church. It was made by John Essex, marbler; William Austen, bronze-founder or latoner; Thomas Stevyns, coppersmith; and a Dutchman, Bartholomew Lambespring, a goldsmith who was responsible for the gilding. Austen was paid for the effigy (excluding the cost of workmen and carriage) the sum of £40, and Lambespring received £13 for the gilding. This proportion remained more or less unchanged through the centuries, due to the dangerous nature of the process. 'Fourteen embossed images of lords and ladies in divers vestments called weepers' cost 13*s.* 4*d.* each, and the whole-length figures of angels holding scrolls inscribed *Sit deo laus in gloria defunctis misericordia*, 5*s.*

each. The effigy of the Earl, with a bear and a griffin at his feet, is in armour, lying on its back, the details being exactly and carefully finished. The work occupied twenty-three years, from 1442 to 1465.

A notable example of large sculpture of the Late Gothic period is a copper-gilt statue of the Archangel Michael, seventeen feet in height, the work of Martin van Rode about whom nothing is known apart from his name. This was placed on the top of the spire of the Hôtel de Ville in Brussels in 1454.

The Netherlands early acquired a reputation for the manufacture of fine metalwork, and the bronze and brass of Dinant (now in Belgium) enjoyed a considerable reputation before the eleventh century, to an extent that the word *dinanderie* became a generic term for work of this kind. The town was also a centre for the distribution of raw materials, selling both copper and calamine, while the local deposits of refractory clay were especially suitable for the

Ill. 81

making of crucibles. In the fourteenth century migratory workmen started similar industries in Brussels, Tournay, Huy, and Middelburg. The products of Dinant were made by casting, hammering into shape, and by cutting and soldering sheet metal. Both fine embossed work, and that produced by hammering sheet metal into *intaglio* moulds was produced, and the Dinant craftsmen were good chisellers and engravers. The chief workmen set themselves up in individual *ateliers* with apprentices and assistants, although there is no record of anything approaching factory organization. The workmen of Dinant met an increasing demand especially for domestic utensils of metal, and hammering as a method of fashioning was in common use. Kettles, cauldrons, saucepans, ewers, basins, and mortars were made in large numbers, although few have survived. Lighting appliances were especially numerous – chandeliers and candelabra – and inscriptions in Platt-Deutsche are fairly common. Dinant itself was captured by Philip the Good in 1466, and the workmen then emigrated elsewhere in the Netherlands, to Germany,

82 (*left*) Reliquary of engraved and gilded brass with the subject of Abraham sacrificing Isaac. Lower Saxony. Eleventh to twelfth century. The technique of engraving is to be seen also in the later sepulchral brasses.

83 Rubbing of a sepulchral brass from Wensley, Yorkshire. Late fourteenth century. The earliest record of a brass of this kind in England was that of Simon de Beauchamp of 1208. This has now disappeared.

to France, and even to England. During the nineteenth century much degenerate Dutch brasswork imitating older styles was exported, crudely embossed work perhaps being the most common. The metal has a reddish-coppery colour instead of the brassy colour of early work.

Chiselling and engraving in the medieval period is to be noticed on such things as the early engraved plates which were fixed to a foundation of wood to make caskets and reliquaries, and on the memorial brasses (of which a rubbing is illustrated) that exist in much greater numbers in England than on the Continent, principally because many of those on the mainland have been destroyed. In England they occur from the twelfth century onwards, some nineteenth-century examples being a product of the Gothic revival of that time. An excellent indication of a Continental origin, however, is to be found in the name 'Cullen plate' (i.e. Cologne plate) given to the imported sheet brass employed in their manufacture. The alloy usually contains about seventy-five per cent of copper and twenty per cent of zinc in the form of calamine, the remainder being tin and lead. The metal itself was very commonly termed 'latten' (O.F. *laiton*). The usual method of engraving the plates was by chiselling, and parts are sometimes additionally ornamented with *champlevé* enamel. Imported Flemish brasses occur in East Anglian chapels, and some English brasses were no doubt the work of immigrant craftsmen.

Ill. 83

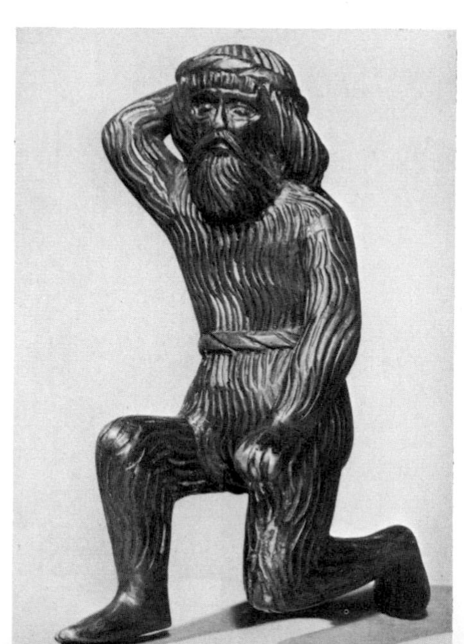

84 A *woodwose* – a wood-spirit or wild man, a hairy denizen of the German forests who symbolized the flesh as opposed to the spirit. German. Fifteenth century.

CHAPTER FOUR

The bronzes of Asia

Bronze employed for the making of ritual vessels appears quite suddenly in China about the middle of the second millennium BC. Surviving specimens excavated in large numbers begin with the Shang dynasty (*c.* 1523–1028 BC).

Until recently the archaeology of China was largely based on literary records and the depredations of grave-robbers, since Chinese official circles were reluctant to permit controlled digging. The picture has been changing for several decades, although not a great deal of information is yet available. For this reason the great bronze vases reached the West clandestinely. Grave-robbing has always been a lucrative pastime in China. It flourished in the Han dynasty (206 BC–AD 221), and as long ago as the eighth century of our era an Arab merchant, Abu Zeid el-Hasan, noted that 'valuables have ceased to be buried with the dead because they are no longer safe from thieves'.

According to Chinese legend the Yellow Emperor, Huang-ti (*fl.* *c.* 2700 BC) was the first to study the art of bronzeworking. He brought order to the warring tribes, subduing the Hsiung-nu (the nomadic Huns), and he is reputed to have fought with a warrior from the south who had 'a bronze skull and an iron forehead'. This is obviously some kind of helmet, and the reference to iron is anachronistic. No Chinese helmets have been discovered which predate the Shang period. Nearer to historic times was Yü the Great (2205–1766 BC), who founded the Hsia dynasty and was the Chinese Cadmus, introducing many of the arts of civilization into China. By tradition Yü cast nine great tripod cauldrons (*li*) from metal obtained from the Nine Provinces which were preserved until the third century. One is to be found as part of a relief sculpture in Shantung, which depicts an attempt to recover the tripods from a river into which they had fallen.

85 (*left*). *Yü*, or wine-vessel, with a swing-handle usually terminating in animal heads, as here. The square *yü* is very unusual. Most are circular in section. Shang dynasty. 1523–1028 BC.

86. A very rare vessel which seems to represent a man being devoured by a tiger, but the animal is much more likely to be a protective spirit, and it is possibly the totem of a clan. China. Shang dynasty.

Literary references suggest that these cauldrons were decorated with the *t'ao t'ieh* mask, and this is one of the most persistent and ubiquitous of Chinese decorative motifs, which is frequently present on archaizing objects in various materials almost to the present day. The term does not occur in literary records before the Han dynasty, and it has never been translated satisfactorily. One version is shown here, but there are many varieties. *Ill. 1*

The appearance of the *t'ao t'ieh* resembles certain totem masks still to be found among the indigenous inhabitants of north-west America, especially in the region of the Bering Straits, whence comes the top of a slate-box with a remarkably similar motif. Basically it is a stylized animal head split down the centre from the back as far as *Ill. 88*

87. *Fang-i*, a bronze vessel magnificently patinated. It was probably used for food-offerings. Shang dynasty.

the nose and opened out. The various elements – eyes, ears, horns, and so forth – lie on either side of the central point represented by the tip of the nose.

Ills. 85, 87 The series of magnificent bronze altar-vessels, of which some are illustrated, seem to have had an almost exclusively religious connotation during the Shang dynasty and the early part of the following Chou dynasty (1028–249 BC), but they came to be employed increasingly for secular purposes, and were probably marks of distinction conferred by the powerful on their followers during the first millennium, as the numerous inscriptions show. Noblemen were allowed a number of bronze vessels varying in size and kind, and they undoubtedly became a kind of insignia of rank to such an extent that it is fairly safe to say that before the end of the Chou period they had largely lost their ritual significance.

The forms of the bronze vessels which first occur during the Shang dynasty have persisted almost down to our own day for vessels of bronze, porcelain, and jade, and it is amusing to notice modern European pottery and porcelain vases based on some of these ancient forms. No significant correspondences seem to exist between the early bronzes and the art of countries further west,

88. Front of a recent slate box with a design representing a monster by the Haida people of the Canadian North Pacific coast. Its resemblance to the *t'ao t'ieh* mask of ancient China is striking (*Ill. 1*). After Boas.

89. Wine-vessel (*yü*) with high-relief decoration representing an owl. China. Shang-Yin dynasty.

although there are distinct resemblances between some of the decorative motifs and the general body of Pacific art – the western seaboard of pre-Columbian America and even the Maoris of New Zealand.

The *t'ao t'ieh* occurs more frequently than any other single motif, and it was probably a protective guardian against evil spirits, a function which even extends to the vase illustrated here. The animals represented include the dragon, tiger, buffalo, ram, bear, stag, and owl, as well as others more difficult to identify. The dragon in China is a beneficent animal controlling rainfall and fertility, as well as being the insignia of the emperor. The elements of the *t'ao t'ieh* mask, sometimes in high relief, are set against a background ornament of which the *lei wên* ('cloud and thunder' fret) is the commonest. In appearance it resembles the Greek key fret, although it also occurs in spiral form.

Ill. 89

90. *Tsun*, or wine-vessel, in the form of an elephant. The animal form is the rarest kind of *tsun*, the more usual variety being a vase of baluster form decorated with a *t'ao t'ieh* mask round the centre. China. Chou dynasty 1028–249 BC.

The earliest specimens are ornamented in a linear style with no very pronounced relief decoration, but an exaggeratedly high relief occurs towards the end of the Shang dynasty and persists into the early part of the Chou dynasty. A return to low relief followed, and this was accompanied by an increasingly naturalistic treatment of animals under the influence of animal bronzes made by nomads dwelling in the Ordos Desert, who achieved a very high level with small plaques. This tendency is especially noticeable during the final part of the Chou dynasty, known as the Period of the Warring States (*c.* 485–201 BC), and it was developed during the Han dynasty, when a bronze wine-jar of baluster form known as a *hu* was sometimes decorated with a frieze depicting a hunting subject usually termed the 'flying gallop'.

91. A pair of chariot lynch-pins (for securing the wheels) in the form of human figures. China. Ninth to sixth century BC.

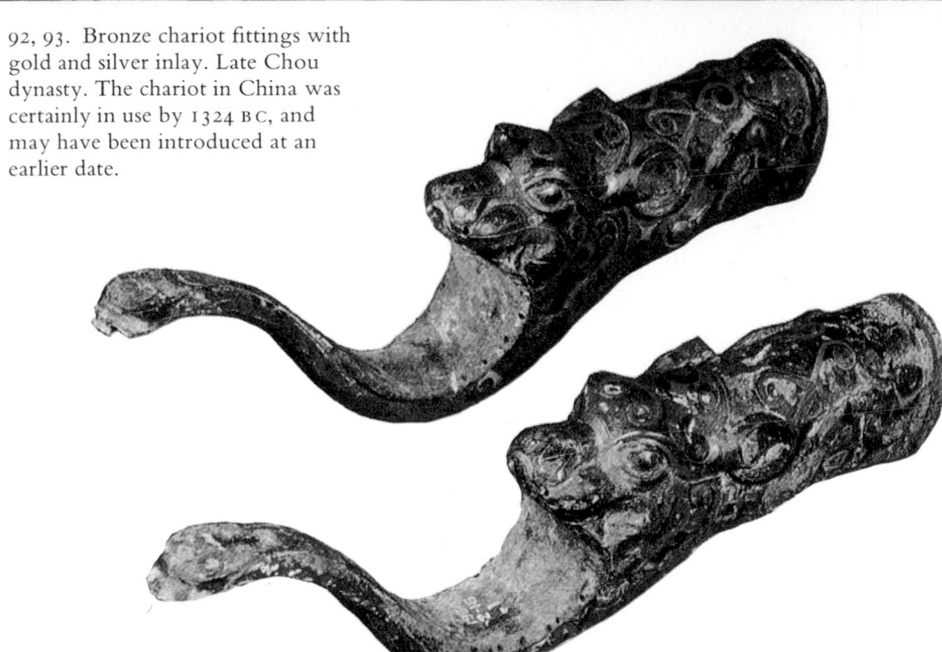

92, 93. Bronze chariot fittings with gold and silver inlay. Late Chou dynasty. The chariot in China was certainly in use by 1324 BC, and may have been introduced at an earlier date.

The revival of ornament in low relief lent itself to inlaying in a variety of substances – gold, silver, copper, turquoise, malachite, and even lacquer. Added decoration to the bronze surface again came into favour during the much later Ming dynasty (AD 1368–1644), but this time in the form of enamels, either *champlevé* (that is, deposited in cells scooped from the surface) or *cloisonné*, the enamel being retained by wires soldered to the surface. This, however, was a technique derived from the West, probably from Byzantium.

Colossal bronze statuary is not found in China today, although it seems to have existed in former times. Literary records refer to twelve statues fifty feet in height cast at the order of Shih Huang-ti (221–206 BC), the Emperor who built the Great Wall and caused the books of former times to be burned, and two of these still survived in the fourth century AD. A few small figures have recently

been found in tombs in Honan Province belonging to the Period of the Warring States, and some late Chou animal figures point to a tradition of figure-making from a still earlier date.

It is known that Tung Cho, a Han emperor of the second century AD, melted many bronze statues then in Lo-yang and Ch'ang-an for coinage, and I think we are justified in assuming that Chinese bronze sculpture of relatively large size, almost certainly cast in sections, was once more common than has been supposed.

Verifiable knowledge of Chinese sculpture begins with the introduction of Buddhism in AD 67. A legend of 121 BC says that during the reign of the Emperor Wu the famous general, Chang Ch'ien, pursued Mongol raiders far into the deserts of Turkestan,

94 (*left*). Table-leg in bronze (one of a pair) inlaid with gold and silver. The form is that of a fantastic monster, and inlaid designs of the period are recognizably the inspiration of those of the later lion *(Ill. 105)*. Late Chou dynasty. *c.* fifth to fourth century BC.

95 (*above*). Bronze figures of Mongolian ponies. China. Chou dynasty. The horse, motive-power of the nomad, was also the subject of some of the finest things in Chinese art. The sacrifice of horses, a nomad custom, was observed in China during the Shang dynasty.

96 (*right*). Bear of gilt-bronze. China. Han dynasty. 206 BC – AD 221. A well-observed example of an animal often represented at the time; it occurs, for instance, as the feet of certain pottery jars.

97. Maitreya (the Buddha-to-come) in gilt-bronze. Wei dynasty. 316–581.

98 (*right*). Buddha, the right hand raised bestowing protection (*abhaya mudra*). Romano-Buddhist sculpture from Gandhara. Sixth to seventh century AD.

and there found some golden (that is, gilt-bronze) images ten feet high, which were brought back and set up in the Emperor's palace. Of these we know nothing for certain, although it is possible to make intelligent guesses, but in AD 316 the Tatars (nomadic Huns and Mongols) established themselves in northern China, founding the Wei dynasty, and, beginning in 338 with a Sakyamuni now in Chicago, a series of gilded bronze statues, sometimes dated and obviously influenced by Graeco-Buddhist work from Gandhara on the Indian north-west frontier, continues through the fifth century and beyond. They were no doubt employed by Buddhist missionaries to convert the Chinese, and the veneration with which they were regarded may be deduced from the tradition that no girl could become an Empress of the Wei without knowing how to cast a bronze figure.

A digression testifying to the skill of the Chinese as bronze-workers is appropriate at this point. Needham describes in detail a bronze seismograph made by Cheng Hêng, mathematician and astronomer, in AD 132 which was so delicately poised that it indicated the direction of earthquake shocks many miles distant and otherwise imperceptible. Excellent cross-bow locks with a trigger action date from the same period, and it is probable that the Chinese reached a high degree of skill in making objects of utility which have since been lost.

During the Sui dynasty (AD 561–618), and especially during the following T'ang dynasty (AD 618–906), there was an increasing tendency to turn to naturalistic ornament, and the arrival of craftsmen from Sassanid Persia fleeing from the armies of Islam brought new influences with them, to be seen both in metalwork and pottery. During the T'ang dynasty some exceptionally fine bronze mirrors were made, although the first mirrors to be recovered date back to Chou times.

Bronze vessels of the Sung dynasty are difficult to date accurately. This period, from 960 to 1279, was, like the preceding T'ang dynasty, one of the great epochs of Chinese art, but it was otherwise a time of strife. The Imperial collections of bronze vessels were destroyed when the Court fled southwards before an invasion of the Mongols, and this led to the copying of ancient bronzes. During the twelfth century the *Hsüan Ho Po Ku Tu Lu* by Wang Fu, a treatise in thirty books illustrated by cuts of ancient bronzes which has often been reprinted, inspired many copies, but the illustrations are inaccurate, and variations in the interpretation of ancient ornament often suggest the correct period for some existing copies. The custom of artificially patinating bronzes in imitation of those of the Shang and Chou dynasties is first to be observed at this time.

The destruction of ancient vessels actually began in 995 when Shih Tsung ordered all bronze vases and figures in private hands to be delivered up for melting, and in 1155 many more ancient vessels were melted. A similar holocaust occurred during the thirteenth century, with the result that, of the bronzes now existing, almost none have survived which have been above ground since

99. Altar-piece, date equivalent to AD 593, made during the Sui dynasty (561–618). Chinese. The central figure is of Buddha on a lotus throne. The two flanking figures represent Avalokiteshvara (later to become Kuan Yin in China) and Mohastamaprapta – Compassion and Wisdom respectively.

their original manufacture, and therefore all should show signs of burial.

Little in the way of bronze vessels was made during the Mongol Yüan dynasty (1280–1368), and Soame Jenyns observes of Ming bronzes that zinc was first added to the alloy during this period. Some bronzes apparently belonging to the fifteenth century have a brown patination with golden glints, perhaps indicative of an alloy which might properly be called brass rather than bronze. The high quality of the bronzes associated with the reign of Hsüan-tê (1426–35) of the Ming dynasty has always been recognized in China, and this reign-mark appears on many specimens rather as commendation than as an indication of date. The colouring of the surface artificially was much practised at this time, but archaizing ornament, such as the *t'ao t'ieh*, is very degenerate and sometimes hardly recognizable. Archaizing bronzes are to be seen again during the Ch'ing dynasty (1644–1912), and most were made in the early years of the reign of Ch'ien Lung (1736–95).

100. A bronze sarcophagus originally gilded, made in six detachable sections. The inner coffin-lid has been repaired. The decoration is in low relief, applied relief, and in the round. The patina is green and black with reddish incrustations. China. T'ang dynasty. 618–906.

The skill of the Chinese bronzeworker in casting large quantities of metal is aptly illustrated by the Great Bell of Peking, reputed to weigh sixty-five tons. This was cast in the reign of Yung-lo (1403–24), and it is related that the first attempts to cast it by the cannon-founder, Kuan Yu, were unsuccessful. One of Yung-lo's daughters, Ko-ai, sacrificed herself by throwing herself into the crucible just as the metal started to flow, leaving behind her shoe in the hand of an attendant who tried to restrain her. The bell was cast successfully, but when it was struck its deep note was followed by a wailing sound in which the word *hsieh* could be heard. It was Ko-ai wailing for her lost shoe.

The technique employed by the Chinese to cast their vessels in the early period cannot be precisely determined. Three methods have been suggested – the use of piece-moulds taken from a prototype of carved wood or pottery; the lost wax technique; and the use either of founders' sand or a clinging loam.

At first it was assumed that the lost wax method was the one adopted, and it would have been quite possible to cast any of the known vessels in this way. Founders' sand can be dismissed without further discussion, if only because a great deal of the fine detail, such as the *lei wên*, could not have been reproduced by this method. The employment of a suitable refractory clay, however, would have presented no difficulty to a people who were already accomplished potters accustomed, even at this early date, to fire to high temperatures. About ten thousand vessels still survive, and this suggests that they must have been made in enormous quantities, perhaps almost on a mass-production basis. The Chinese were, of course, the original inventors of the production-line, which was extensively used for the making of porcelain in the seventeenth century of our own era.

A combination of hardwood prototypes and moulds of plaster mixed with a refractory material is a possibility, although favourable evidence is scanty. Willetts writes of a composite material found at An-yang which bore a negative pattern of bronze design, but says nothing of its nature. Limestone and marble, common in China, are obvious sources of plaster.

101. Bronze open-work mount from the Caucasus with an animal subject. Scythian. *c.* fifth century BC.

Only pottery prototypes and mould-sections have hitherto been recovered, but this does not entirely exclude the use of wood as a prototype, since pottery is permanent and wood which is buried rapidly decays. As to their ability to fire a pottery mould to a high enough temperature, there is evidence for this in a vessel from the An-yang period (1400–1100 BC) in Washington's Freer Gallery, which must have been fired at about 1100° C.

It is impossible here to examine all the possibilities in detail, and the interested reader is referred to Noel Barnard's *Bronze Casting in Ancient China* (Australian National University, 1961) for a discussion of the technical aspects. Here it is only possible to say that the discovery of sectional moulds of pottery suggests that the lost wax technique was not employed at this time.

103 (*right*). An ibex, a lively small bronze in the Sino-Siberian animal style of the fifth to first centuries BC which influenced the Chinese bronze style of the Late Chou and former Han dynasties.

102 (*above*). Pole-finial in the form of an ibex head. Sino-Siberian. Fifth to first centuries BC. The animal may be the totem of a clan. Pole-finials occur also in China during the Shang and Chou dynasties.

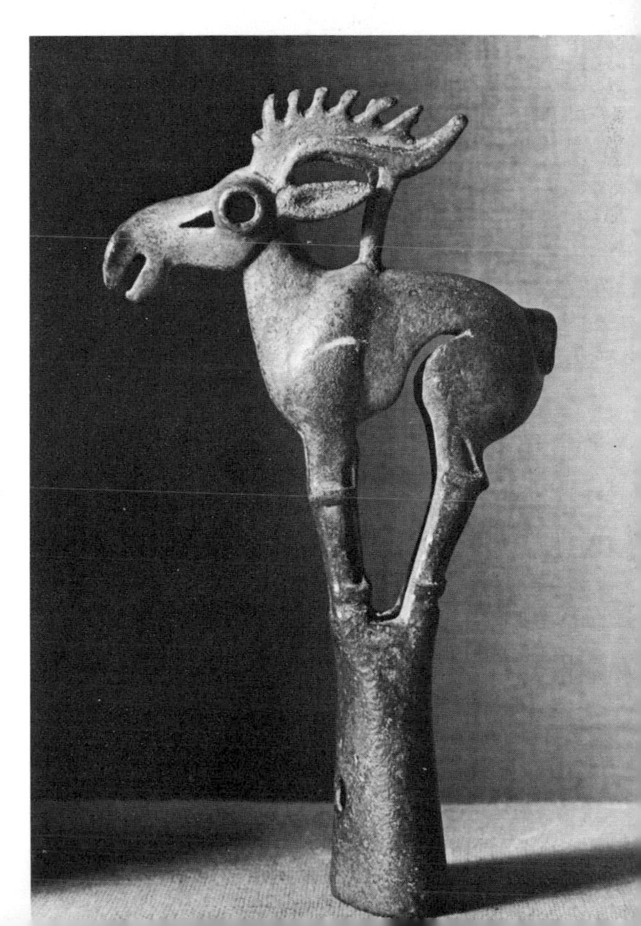

104 (*right*). Pole-finial in the form of an elk from the Ordos Desert, contemporary with the Han dynasty in China. *c.* second to first century BC.

The soil of China is much kinder to buried bronze than that of many other regions, and excavated objects are not only often in surprisingly good condition, but the patination induced by burial is extremely colourful. It is highly valued both for its appearance and as evidence of age, and it should not be lightly tampered with, although removal is justified when an inscription or inlaying is suspected. Later bronzes, some almost modern, have been given fake patination which is a colourable imitation of the products of corrosion. The amount and type of corrosion varies from place to place, but instances of the metallic nature of the alloy being completely lost are rare, and most Shang bronzes have no more than a surface corrosion.

The alloys employed were variable in their constituents in relation to intended use. Tools and weapons for instance usually contain a standard amount of about ninety per cent of copper to ten per cent of tin, whereas mirrors contain about fifty per cent of each, which is the best alloy for the purpose.

Early Japanese bronzes have not been studied in such detail as those from China, but there is ample evidence that a high degree of skill had been achieved by the opening of the present era. By the Nara period (AD 710–94) work in gilded copper was of very high quality, and this period, approximately contemporary with the T'ang dynasty in China, is perhaps to be compared with it for general excellence.

The art of metalwork received considerable impetus from the introduction of Buddhism in 552, when the King of Korea sent Buddhist images to the Japanese Emperor, and during the Asuka period (AD 673–710) the influence of India arrived in Japan by way of T'ang China.

Early work in gilded bronze and copper includes embossed and pierced plaques, especially during the Nara period, which were used to adorn the wooden structures of temples. At this time the Japanese

105. Bronze figure of a winged lion inlaid with gold and silver. Sung dynasty (AD 960–1279). The inlaid motifs decorating this vigorously modelled little creature are closely based on those of the latter part of the Chou dynasty (*Ill. 94*).

excelled at the making of sheet copper. Altar-vessels, elaborately pierced lanterns for temple courtyards (the oldest and finest perhaps being the work of an eighth-century Chinese craftsman at Nara), and Buddhist figures of fine workmanship, all testify to the progress made.

Nara was, at this time, the capital of Japan, and it is here that the Shoso-in Pavilion is situated, within the bounds of the Todaiji Monastery. This contains a remarkable collection of art-treasures of all kinds presented by the Dowager Empress in 756 which had been assembled by the Emperor Shomu. Although it has received subsequent additions it is, without doubt, the oldest art-collection in the world still to be preserved intact.

In the grounds of the Monastery is a statue of the Buddha, the *Daibutu*, erected in 752 and consecrated by Shomu, which is especially worthy of note. The height is fifty-three feet, the face nine feet in breadth, and the eye almost four feet wide. The bronze has a thickness of six inches at its maximum, and it contains about two hundred tons of metal. We have the authority of Professor Gowland for saying that it is the largest example of soldering in the world, the solder being an alloy of tin and lead. The body, and the greater part of the lotus on which it rests, is formed of plates measuring about ten inches by twelve, but the more modern parts are much larger and not soldered. The head fell off during a fire, and the present head dates from the sixteenth century. The surface is gilded with mercury, a process which the Japanese seem to have acquired from the Chinese since this metal was not known in Japan at the time. The metal of which the statue is formed is the *karakane* alloy, which contains copper, tin, and lead, and is later discussed.

Several more of these colossal statues of the Buddha are to be found in Japan, some in bronze, and the last of them, forty-eight

106. The Buddha of Healing with a flame nimbus. Gilt-bronze. Late seventh century A.D. From Nara, Japan, cast between 697 and 710. Nara was the capital of the Empire from the fifth century to the beginning of the eighth.

107. The Great Buddha. Kamakura, Japan. This thirteenth-century figure is the second largest in Japan, the largest being at Nara. The method of casting in poured sections is quite plainly to be seen. Kamakura was the centre of national life from the end of the twelfth century till the middle of the fourteenth.

feet in height, was erected at Hyogo in 1891, paid for by a pious paper manufacturer.

The Edo period is remarkable for magnificent works in bronze, and at Nikko – subject of the saying, 'Do not use the word "magnificent" until you have seen Nikko' – is the Mausoleum of the Shogun Ieyashu (1542–1616), with a fine gateway and other works in bronze, including a Dutch candelabrum brought to Japan by traders. The tomb itself, shaped like a pagoda, is a single casting of an alloy said to contain gold, and it is provided with a pair of gates of which the roof is a solid casting. On either side of the gates are two bronze lions of Fo (Buddha). Engelbrecht Kaempfer (1657–1716), a Dutch traveller who was in Japan in 1683, commented on the skill of Japanese craftsmen in metalwork of all kinds, but by the eighteenth century colossal statues and architectural bronzework had become an antiquarian taste, and objects such as the *okimono* had become the rule.

The distinguishing mark of the *okimono* is that it has no practical use. The word is difficult to translate, but it appears to mean an object for a special place, which is usually the raised platform on which it is displayed. The *okimono* is not necessarily of bronze. Most are incense-burners (*koro*), flower-vases, figures of dragons and other supernatural creatures, living animals (deer, fish, crabs, crayfish, tortoises, and so forth), and figures of immortals and gods. Objects which can be placed in this category are rare in the West, and are too much in the Japanese taste to have appealed to travellers of former times, although they are now accorded greater appreciation.

Household utensils in bronze are fairly common, and decorated with excellent taste, but especially treasured in Japan are the various items of sword-furniture, on the decoration of which great skill and ingenuity was lavished. These comprise the *kashira* or pommel cap, the *tsuba* or guard, and the *fuchi* of flattened oval form which encircled the blade at the top of the *ricasso* where it joins the hilt. Usually of iron or steel, *tsuba* are sometimes of bronze, and sometimes of iron damascened with bronze, gold, and silver. *Tsuba* isolated from the swords for which they were made are collected in Japan, and latterly in Europe.

The peculiar genius of the Japanese bronzesmith lies in novel techniques of inlaying and colouring, of which a lobster-red patina to copper which is very difficult to attain is an example. A technique known as *mokume* (literally, wood-grain) required several sheets of differently coloured alloys to be brazed together, scored with heavy cuts, and partially drilled. This was then hammered flat, bringing the underlying colours to the surface in a manner suggestive of figured wood, with wavy lines and knot-like markings. The surface was sometimes raised from the back in slight bosses which were then filed flat, leaving a pattern of differently coloured alloys with an effect not unlike chalcedony. Artificially coloured Japanese bronzes should not be polished with abrasive cleaners which may destroy the surface effect, but washed in soap and water and carefully dried.

The Japanese have always paid great attention to alloys. Lead is the significant inclusion in *karakane* bronzes, which were especially easy to pour and therefore often used for large castings. Small quantities of zinc (say three or four per cent) are not unusual, but the addition of fifteen per cent to make something like a true brass did not occur before the eighteenth century, and even then it usually contained five or six per cent of lead. *Sentoku*, containing up to thirteen per cent of zinc, may have been used in the fifteenth century, and legend has it that vessels of this kind also contained gold, although this metal has not, I think, ever been identified in it. Japanese taste generally prefers gilded copper or bronze to brass. *Shakudo* does contain up to five per cent of gold, in some cases with a little silver, but it is mostly copper. The gold gives a black surface with violet tones. *Shibuichi* contains about half copper and half silver, but the proportions vary. It was patinated artificially to obtain a handsome grey. *Shibuichi* was much used for sword-furniture after the seventeenth century, and it was also employed by the Mint in place of silver to debase the coinage.

Generally, Japanese bronzes have a low melting-point owing to the frequent inclusion of lead. Partly this was due to the vogue for large works, some of which were cast *in situ*, and partly to the poor refractory qualities of the fireclay from which the moulds were made. There was, apparently, difficulty in procuring the highly refractory clays most suitable for casting a normal copper-tin alloy.

Japanese art is still often underestimated in the West. This is partly the fault of the Japanese themselves. During the nineteenth century they pandered to debased Western taste by making tawdry and meretricious objects, such as large vases with dragons in high relief writhing round them, especially for Western consumption. In general, their own preferences for simplicity and asymmetry of design, allied to exceptional technical skill, produced works which will bear comparison with those from most other places.

The bronzes of the Indus Valley reveal an excellent knowledge of metalworking, and the skill of the Indian people as bronzeworkers has survived until the present day in the villages, where the casting of statuettes is still a village craft.

108. Hunting-group. Primitive Indian bronze made by traditional methods in one of the villages. Nineteenth century. Even today the casting of bronze ornaments by the lost wax method is still carried on.

The Aryan invaders of India came in chariots, which is evidence of a fairly high level of metalworking, to be found among most nomadic tribes of the time, and they used bronze swords and weapons. Little has survived from this period, however. There seems to have been some use of the lost wax method of casting at Taxila, where Alexander the Great halted before his battle with Porus in 326 BC, and both Greek and Roman influences lingered long afterwards on the north-west frontier at Ghandara, to travel thence to China.

The earliest Buddha images certainly belong to the first century BC, and are perhaps older, and from the eighth century to the twelfth of our era large numbers were made in gilt-bronze with the familiar flame-like nimbus.

Non-Buddhist Indian sculpture was greatly influenced by the dance, and, as in Indian painting, poses were commonly drawn from the elaborate vocabulary of gesture which formed the narrative

109. Hanuman, the monkey god, from a Vaishnara shrine. Ceylon. Eleventh century or later.

110 (*right*). *Siva Nataraja* (Siva as Lord of the Dance). Madras. Late Chola style. *c.* twelfth century AD. There was a considerable revival of metal sculpture during the Chola period (ninth to thirteenth centuries). All are cast by the lost wax technique and are solid.

content of Indian dancing. Sculptured figures are, as it were, frozen at a significant point in one or other of the ritual dances. Erotic emphasis is common, and in this Indian art more nearly resembles a good deal of the art of the West rather than that of the Far East. It is remarkable that certain early Buddhist scriptures proscribe the curious crime of sexual intercourse with statues of goddesses, which I think is unique.

The great contribution of Indian bronzework is the rendering of active movement in a way which is graceful and credible without being absurd. How difficult this is may be seen from contemplation of the Roman copy of the Greek *Laocoön* which is conspicuously unsuccessful in avoiding this pitfall. Characteristic of Indian female figures is an exaggerated emphasis of the sexual attributes – narrow waists, generously proportioned buttocks, and breasts of truly transatlantic amplitude – which is contrary to the almost asexual nature of most Buddhist sculpture.

No large figures were made as a general rule, although one over seven feet in height has been recorded. This was apparently cast in two pourings, one over the other, the first perhaps acting as a core. This technique has no parallel elsewhere.

The finest bronzes have an air of sensual luxury, and are sometimes engraved, finely chiselled, and inlaid with precious metals. The practice of insetting precious and semi-precious stones dates from the fifteenth century, and most such work originated in Nepal.

The influence of Chinese and northern Mongol art is evident in some Nepalese work, as well as in the bronzes of Tibet most of which were produced in Lhasa by Nepalese craftsmen. Little or nothing is known of bronzeworking in Tibet before the eighteenth century, but large figures of gilt-bronze were made for the temples, one source estimating 'several yards high'. Many-armed figures were built up partly by casting and partly by using beaten plates, and inlaying with precious stones was common. Embossed work of good quality is to be seen in vessels of all kinds such as tea-pots and tea-containers, and plaques of gilt-bronze, often pierced and covered with a profusion of orderly decorative elements, are also to be noted. Embossed work, in fact, seems to have been a Tibetan speciality. Dating is extremely difficult apart from specific evidence.

Excellent Buddhist sculpture has come from South-east Asia, and specimens, usually fragmentary, are not uncommon in the West, of which a near life-size head of Buddha belonging to the eighteenth century is the most often seen.

The Near and Middle East alternately formed a bridge and a barrier to Western trade with the Far East with the rise and fall of empires and incursions of the nomads under a long succession of leaders, such as the eleventh-century invasion of the Seljuk Turks under Toghrul Beg, followed by the Mongols of Genghis Khan and Tamerlane. Craftsmen on several occasions were dispersed eastward and westward, especially during the invasion of Persia by Islamic armies in the seventh century, when Sasanid craftsmen took the influence of Persia with them to China and Byzantium.

The ancient skills of the Persians enjoyed a revival during the period of Sasanid rule, which began in AD 227 and ended with the defeat of Persian armies at Nihavand in 641. Metalworking was not slow to reflect this revival. Embossed work is excellent in quality, and ewers and rhytons handsomely decorated with animals and conventional foliage are exceptionally important objects. The ewers were much prized in China, where their graceful forms were later reproduced in porcelain. Rhytons are among the finest examples of the metalwork of the period, but they have been the subject of forgery. Sasanian art, widely sought from China to the Atlantic seaboard, played a not inconsiderable part in the development of Byzantine art and medieval styles further west.

The Mohammedan Arabs were as destitute of culture as some of the nomads who had come from the east, and they absorbed that of the peoples they conquered. They also profoundly affected the art of metalwork. Hitherto speculation about the nature of metals, the ways in which they differed from other substances, had been relatively slight, and little attention was paid to their strict classification.

111. Standard-head (?). Luristan. *c.* sixth century BC. It may represent Gilgamesh struggling with two monsters, but the symbolism is extremely obscure.

112. Head of an ibex. Furniture-mount. Persian. Achaemenid period. Sixth to fifth century BC.

113. Horse-furniture. Cheek-pieces in the form of partly-human, horned and winged quadrupeds, reminiscent of the colossal cherubim which guarded Assyrian palace entrances. Luristan. *c.* 500 BC.

Metals possessed properties peculiar to themselves which could be exploited in a variety of ways, but methods of working them were entirely empirical. Systematic investigation began in Alexandria in the first century of the present era, and the Arabs were the inheritors of Greek and Alexandrian speculation on these and kindred subjects when the libraries of the ancient world fell into their hands. The Nestorian Christians, who had interested themselves in these subjects, journeyed eastwards, ultimately to China, taking their knowledge and manuscripts with them.

The art of alchemy was subsequently established at Baghdad fostered by the Abbasid Caliphs, and Arabic became the language of scientific inquiry, a fact to which the many loan-words current in European scientific vocabularies testify. Arab researches reached Europe by way of Moorish Spain, where treatises were translated by Jewish scholars, and in this way knowledge of metalworking in its technical aspects was improved both in Europe and the East.

114. Bronze bust of a king of the Sasanid period (AD 226–641). Persian. Probably seventh century. The Sasanids were involved in an almost continuous struggle with Byzantium in the west and the nomads in the east.

The inlaying of copper and bronze with the precious metals, a characteristic Islamic technique, appears to date from the twelfth century, perhaps originating at Mosul on the Tigris. What seems to be the earliest dated example (in Leningrad) was made in 1148. Work of this kind became very widely distributed, and it was often associated with finely-detailed pierced work. The rise of Cairo as a metalworking centre can be dated to about the middle of the thirteenth century with the fall of the Mamluk Sultans, and large ewers, bowls, caskets, candlesticks, furniture-mounts, inlaid plates for doors, and richly ornamented covers for the Koran were all made and sold in the Suk el-Keftiyin, *keft* being the term for inlaying copper vessels with silver and gold. Writing in 1420 El-Maqrizi says 'the demand for inlaid copperwork has fallen off in our time, and for many years people have turned away from buying what was to be had of it'.

Metalworking in the Middle East enjoyed a temporary revival under Shah Abbas (acceded 1586, d. 1628), when work of excellent quality was produced, a good deal of it inspired by Islamic inlaid work. Some objects of copper were tinned to simulate silver, a deceit practised by the Gauls in Roman Imperial times which has continued to this day in the Near East. In modern times workshops for making forgeries of Luristan and Sasanian metalwork have been established in Persia, notably near Hamadan, of which the best are good enough to have been included in exhibitions of Persian art.

115. This inlaid brass ewer bearing a date equivalent to AD 1232 is characteristic of much Islamic metalwork of the period. From Mosul, in northern Mesopotamia. The technique has been imitated in a debased form in more recent times.

CHAPTER FIVE

The Renaissance to the end of the sixteenth century

To think of the Renaissance in Italy strictly as a revival of the traditions of the Classical world would not be entirely true. This could more accurately be said of the northern countries where, for nearly three centuries, the Gothic style had completely vanquished the remnants of Classicism, and it was there that Italian modes, and the new spirit of inquiry abroad in the world of art and letters, took root and flourished as soon as the seed had been sown. But the plant was already well nourished in Italian soil, where Gothic had been largely regarded with some distaste as barbarous and alien.

Nevertheless, even in Italy the appearance of a new impetus is marked; fresh life was infused into old traditions and new departures were inspired. The year 1204 marks the arrival of Byzantine craftsmen fleeing from the sack of the city by Crusaders, and a similar influx took place in 1453 when the city was captured by the Ottoman Turks under Mahomet II. The influence of Islamic craftsmen must also be taken into account. It can be found sporadically in decorative art of all kinds, principally in textiles, and it occurs both in the south and in Venice which was the principal *entrepôt* of the Eastern trade.

The making of bronze statuary in Italy had languished almost since the fall of the Roman Empire, although the art of casting large quantities of the metal had been preserved by bell-founders, and latterly by cannon-founders. Cannon were frequently considerable works of decorative art, and even in Cellini's day the services of their makers were still in demand, although he thought little of their skill. Times were changing rapidly in the fourteenth century, and battles of the kind to which Machiavelli refers, when a four-hour contest between Florentine and Milanese armoured warriors resulted in a solitary casualty – a man who fell off his horse, were a thing of the past. Military demand for bronze siege-pieces capable of shattering the fortifications of the day undoubtedly contributed to the technical development necessary for the casting of large statuary and in 1452 a Hungarian engineer named Urban produced a cannon for Mahomet II, used during the siege of Byzantium, that was seventeen feet long, weighed as many tons, and threw a stone ball weighing almost half a ton. This was an object of admiration and terror, although by 1523 when the Turks besieged Malta such weapons had become almost commonplace.

Italian sculpture before the fifteenth century had been largely of wood and stone, although infrequent examples of bronze sculpture occur. One is to be found in the cathedral square of Perugia – the Fonte Maggiore, which was erected between 1274 and 1278. Only partly of bronze, it was the work of Nicolo Pisano, his son Giovanni, and a pupil, Arnolfo di Cambio. The bronzework of the Fonte Maggiore was cast by Maestro Rossi of Perugia, but Andrea Pisano (1270–1348), one of Giovanni's pupils, was regarded by Vasari as 'the best exponent [of sculpture] who had until then appeared in Tuscany, especially in the art of bronze-casting'. Andrea probably learned the art from a certain Bertuccius in Venice, a founder who made the gates of the great central doors of St Mark's. So highly was Andrea's skill regarded in Florence that he was entrusted in 1330 with a commission to make bronze doors for the Baptistery of San Giovanni with panels depicting scenes from the life of the Saint. The reliefs were modelled with the assistance of three Florentine goldsmiths and cast for the first time by Maestro Lionardo, the son of a Venetian bell-founder. This attempt was unsuccessful, and the doors were recast under Andrea's own supervision and set up in 1336.

Ills. 116, 117

These doors were the first to be cast by native Italian workmen since Roman days, and they inspired a competition at the beginning of the fifteenth century for another door to surpass the first. Lorenzo

116. The doors which are now the southern gate of the Florentine Baptistery. Commissioned in 1330, Andrea Pisano completed the wax models in three months. The principal difficulty was to cast it, an operation not completed successfully until about 1336.

Ghiberti, Jacopo della Quercia, and Filippo Brunelleschi were among the contenders, and the commission was awarded finally to Ghiberti, who completed the work in twenty-one years, from 1403 to 1424, helped by Donatello and Michelozzo. Trial-pieces for the competition are preserved in the Bargello. These have for their subject Abraham sacrificing Isaac, and the doors were intended to comprise a number of scenes from the Old Testament. The subject was later changed to scenes from the life of Christ in twenty-eight reliefs, and was the first of two such commissions.

Ills. 118, 119

It marks the beginning of an unprecedented development in the art of sculpture. That this development began in Florence is hardly a matter for surprise. It was among the most flourishing of all Italian cities in the fourteenth century, and its merchants had evolved a system of commerce based on its textile industries which laid the foundation for modern economic structures, with crafts and industries organized into Guilds to which all had to belong if they

117. Panel from Andrea Pisano's door in the Gothic style.

were to participate in the government of the State. The Medici bank was only one of those established in the city, although it was the greatest, with branches in a score of European cities, including London. Eventually the family came to dominate the Florentine scene, and they proved to be notable patrons of the arts, no doubt inspired by the art-dealing which was one of the activities of the bank. Cosimo de' Medici the Elder (1389–1464) offered friendship and patronage to artists and men of letters which both attracted and retained men of exceptional ability, of whom, in sculpture, Ghiberti and Donatello were the most influential.

The revival of Classical learning reached Florence in the middle of the fourteenth century, when Boccaccio arrived in the city bringing with him his collection of Greek and Latin manuscripts. This was at a time when the nobility of Rome could find no better use for their ancient buildings than to fortify them against the dissensions of the times, and it was not until the middle of the fifteenth

118. Detail of one of the panels by Ghiberti for the north gate of the Baptistery, Florence. *The scourging of Christ.*

century, with the accession of Pope Nicholas V, that Rome emerged from the dereliction which had overtaken it. From this time onwards, however, increasing enthusiasm for the relics of antiquity is to be found among the occupants of the Papal throne, and the discoveries made in the latter years of that century began profoundly to influence the course of art elsewhere in Italy.

When Ghiberti competed for the commission to make the door for the Baptistery the most important metalworking craft was that of the goldsmith. Ghiberti's stepfather, a noted goldsmith of his day, influenced his stepson's career and technique. Ghiberti himself became a member of the Guild of Goldsmiths in 1409, and only in 1427 did he join the Stonemasons' Guild. Donatello, in his youth, belonged to a circle which included both sculptors and goldsmiths.

It was natural that goldsmiths should flourish. The bankers and industrialists of Florence commissioned works in the precious metals for the same reason that the Romans amassed collections of gold and silver plate. Their tastes generally had much in common with those of the Romans. They liked portraits to resemble the person represented, and they wanted a naturalistic art instead of the old styles to which the Church still clung. Ghiberti's doors like many of his other works, were commissioned by the citizens of Florence and they chose the design they preferred.

Ghiberti's own attachment to the Classical enthusiasms of his day have been questioned. The panels of his first door, for instance, apart from certain qualities of design, are surrounded by quadrilobate mouldings which are essentially Gothic. In this work, however, he was necessarily following the manner of the earlier doors of Andrea Pisano, and there is little doubt that he shared the general contemporary interest in works of Classical antiquity. It was said of him that he was among the first to study ancient sculpture, of which he seems to have assembled a large collection. Ghiberti himself wrote

119. The north gate of the Baptistery by Ghiberti, who was assisted by Donatello and others, is decorated with scenes from the Life of Christ. They were started in 1403 and completed in 1424.

of his second door that he had taken care to observe the rules of proportion 'and, as far as I could, to imitate nature in exact relationships and contours'. Brunelleschi assisted with the perspective of the architectural representations in the panels of the second door and, according to Vasari, helped to polish the reliefs of the first.

While work on his first door was proceeding Ghiberti received a commission from the Guild of Cloth Merchants to execute a statue of St John the Baptist, eight feet high, which, he says, 'was cast in fine bronze and erected in 1414'. This work is among the earliest to reveal the elements of the new Classicism, and it was placed in the Church of Orsanmichele.

Orsanmichele is a remarkable historical record of the progression of style in Italian sculpture during the fifteenth and sixteenth centuries. Originally a granary, the ground floor was converted into a church, completed in 1404, which was, according to the records of the Commune of Florence held to discuss the plans, intended to be of the 'utmost splendour and magnificence'. The upper storey, however, continued to be used as a granary until the middle of the sixteenth century. At intervals round the external walls were set fourteen niches, in each of which was a statue commissioned by one or other of the Guilds. Some of the niches are Gothic in style, while others are Classical and surmounted by a pediment.

To these statues Ghiberti also contributed a *St Stephen* for the Guild of Woollen Weavers, and, in 1420, a *St Matthew* for the Guild of Bankers and Money-changers, a work in which he was assisted by Michelozzo. Donatello contributed a marble *St George* for the Armourers, now replaced by a bronze cast, and a marble *St Peter* for the Guild of Butchers. The last to be commissioned, by the Judges and Notaries, was *St Luke* executed by Giovanni da Bologna in 1602.

While work on the first of Ghiberti's doors for the Florentine Baptistery was in progress he received a commission from the Municipality of Siena for two of the six gilt-bronze reliefs ornamenting the font of the Gothic Baptistery there which were begun in 1417 and finished in 1425. Of the remainder, one is by Jacopo della Quercia, who designed the font, one by Donatello, and two by

120. Ghiberti. *John the Baptist brought before Herod.* Panel from the Baptistery Font, Siena. Commissioned 1417, completed 1425.

Turino di Sano and his son, Giovanni. Those by Ghiberti are the *Baptism of Christ* and *John the Baptist brought before Herod*, the second of which may have been chiselled by Turino the Elder. The vocabulary of Classical ornament is especially noticeable in the second of the two, where the architectural setting modelled in perspective shows swags pendant between ox-skulls, scrolling acanthus at the base of Herod's throne, and semicircular arches replacing the pointed arches of the Gothic style. The slender pillars and their capitals, however, are hardly of Classic proportions.

Ill. 120

The use of perspective in this way, and the employment of Classical ornamental motifs in the rendering of the architectural setting, foreshadows the handling of similar elements decorating the panels of Ghiberti's second door for the Baptistery, called by Michelangelo the 'porte del Paradiso', which was commissioned in 1425. One of the panels, the *Meeting of Solomon with the Queen of Sheba*, is set in a building with pointed arches and Gothic vaulting, although it has pilasters, Corinthian capitals, and pedimented windows. This door, of the same size as Ghiberti's first, was completed in ten square reliefs of scenes from the Old Testament, instead of twenty-eight panels set in two parallel rows, fourteen on each valve, and the work occupied Ghiberti and his assistants for twenty-seven years. These two doors, therefore, spanned most of his working life.

Ill. 121

Baldinucci, writing towards the end of the seventeenth century of the early *John the Baptist*, says that in this work 'Lorenzo, who cast it admirably, . . . had already begun to display signs of the excellent modern style, having been the first to study ancient sculpture . . .', and an increasing comprehension of the Classical style marks Ghiberti's treatment of architectural settings, especially in the panels of his second door.

The panels of both Ghiberti's doors are pictorial in style, a technique not inaptly termed by Symonds 'painting in bronze'. The use of relief on several planes in the modelling of the panels of the second door may also be seen in the principal panel of a reliquary for the Cathedral at Florence, intended to contain the bones of St Zenobius, which Ghiberti completed in 1446, and to this aspect Ghiberti referred when he wrote 'working with the utmost diligence and care, I introduced into some of my compositions as many as a hundred figures, which I modelled on different planes, so that those nearest the eye might appear larger, and those more remote smaller in proportion'. He worked on the second door, in the felicitous words of another nineteenth-century authority, 'with brushes of steel and canvas of bronze'. Brunelleschi discovered the scientific principles underlying the use of perspective some time before 1424, but the date is uncertain and Ghiberti was not acquainted with them when he was working on his first door where his

121. One of the panels of the eastern door of the Baptistery, Florence, by Ghiberti. The *Gates of Paradise*. The Victoria and Albert Museum possesses casts.

occasional use of perspective is of the empirical Roman kind, and one of his panels, the *Adoration of the Magi*, has a figure grossly out of scale in a manner Gothic rather than Classical.

Of Ghiberti's work as a goldsmith nothing now remains, but Cellini was of the opinion that he excelled in minute works rather than large ones – a verdict confirmed by comparison of his large statues with the panels of the doors, which exhibit evidence of his earlier training in the craft.

Ghiberti's sculpture is among the earliest manifestations of the return to the mainstream of European tradition, but it is to Donatello that we must turn for its development, and it may be said of his work that he initiated a new era in the art of sculpture within the framework of this tradition. It is, perhaps, not without significance that quite early in his career he achieved a considerable reputation as a restorer of ancient statuary.

Donato di Niccolò di Betto Bardi, called Donatello, was born in Florence *c.* 1386, and is first recorded as an assistant in Ghiberti's workshop in 1403. His early work is in marble, and in this medium he carved a statue of St Mark for Orsanmichele for the Guild of Linen-weavers, a commission probably completed late in 1412. The marble *St George* for the same place, ordered by the Guild of Armourers, is undocumented, but may have been started before 1417, and his *St Peter* for the Butchers' Guild, the attribution of which has been the subject of controversy, is perhaps of approximately the same period.

The year in which Donatello turned to bronze as a medium cannot be accurately determined, although he was a member of the

122. Donatello. *St Louis of Toulouse*. Gilded bronze. Originally made for Orsanmichele, *c.* 1423, it was removed before 1510 and replaced by Verrocchio's group.

Company of St Luke as a goldsmith and chiseller of metal in 1412. It is perhaps significant that his close association with Michelozzo Michelozzi, architect, sculptor, goldsmith, and bronze-caster, began *c.* 1423, the date of the remarkable *St Louis of Toulouse* in gilded bronze for Orsanmichele, for the niche now occupied by Verrocchio's gilded bronze group *Jesus and Doubting Thomas*, and the partnership is first recorded in 1425. Michelozzo was born in 1396 and had been associated in his early years with Donatello when both assisted Ghiberti. In partnership with Donatello he appears to have assumed responsibility for the architectural design of such joint projects as the Tombs of Pope John XXIII and Cardinal Brancacci.

Ill. 122

For the font at Siena Donatello executed the relief *Herod's Feast* assisted by Michelozzo, in which the treatment of both the architectural details and of perspective is superior to that of Ghiberti. At

Ill. 124

123. Donatello. *David.* Executed about 1430 for the Medici family, this was the first free-standing statue to be made in bronze since ancient times. Vasari's charge that it was a cast from life is without foundation.

a slightly later date, before 1430, Donatello executed two female figures (his first) for the font – *Faith* and *Hope* probably cast by Michelozzo. Three *putti* in the form of angels for the same place are strongly reminiscent of ancient *putti*, a theme to become widely popular later.

Herod's Feast is in the manner of Ghiberti, but in 1435 Donatello was commissioned to make bronze doors for the Sacristy of San

124. Donatello. *Herod's Feast*. 1423–27. Font of the Baptistery of San Giovanni, Siena. Originally given to Jacopo della Quercia, the commission was later awarded to Donatello.

125. Panel from Donatello's door made for the Sacristy of San Lorenzo, Florence.

Lorenzo which Brunelleschi had largely rebuilt for the Medicis on the old site. These doors had for their subject the Apostles and the Martyrs, each of ten panels. Each panel comprises two figures modelled on a plain surface, and this unusual treatment both pictorial and plastic, as well as the dramatic poses of the figures, was much criticized, and seems to have led to a quarrel between the sculptor and Brunelleschi who strongly disapproved. The sometimes vigorous movement of these reliefs certainly mingled uneasily with Brunelleschi's design, and they were at the time an unprecedented innovation.

Ill. 125

Perhaps just before this, between 1430 and 1433, Donatello executed his remarkable bronze *David*, which is now in the Bargello and once stood in the courtyard of the Medici Palace. Its pedestal has been lost. No doubt this bronze, conceived in the spirit of the antique which may be seen even in the adoption of the old Greek shepherd's hat, was inspired by Donatello's access to the Medici collections of Classical statuary and engraved gems. It has been regarded as suggestive of the work of Praxiteles which, in its softly rounded and almost feminine contours perhaps it is, although it hardly conforms strictly to Greek canons. In this work Donatello returned to the nude which, as a subject for sculpture, had been neglected since Classical times, and which in the sixteenth century especially was to become one of the commonest expressions of Renaissance Classicism. Donatello's *David* was the first major work of free-standing sculpture made since the fall of the Roman Empire, and it marks a point of departure which had a profound effect on the subsequent course of the art.

Ill. 123

Another event of comparable significance was Donatello's equestrian statue of the General Erasmo da Narni, the *Gattamelata* or honeyed-cat, which is in the Piazza del Santo at Padua. Donatello's move to Padua took place in 1443, perhaps in consequence of his quarrel with Brunelleschi over the Sacristy doors, and he probably received the commission for the *Gattamelata* monument in 1446.

Ills. 126–8

Gattamelata gained his nickname from an ability to combine an outward show of sweet reasonableness with predatory cunning. He was a leader of *condottieri*, mercenary bands employed by the Italian cities for aggression and defence, and perhaps the greatest honour which could be paid to a leader of this kind was to erect a statue to him, although an Italian city is said to have arranged for the murder of one of them so that he could be honoured as a saint. There had been a few equestrian statues before this one, notably the

126. Erasmo da Narni, the Generale Gattamelata, at Padua by Donatello is much more classically based than *Ill. 129*. It not only influenced North Italian art profoundly, but it was the inspiration of many later equestrian statues.

NATELLI

127. Detail of *Ill. 126*. The resemblance to Roman portraiture is enhanced by the Classical dress of the rider.

much restored *Can Grande della Scala* at Verona and the *Barnabo Visconti* at Milan, but these horses of stone were necessarily stocky, with four sturdy legs firmly implanted on the ground, and with additional supports. Equestrian statues are, in fact, singularly rare in stone because the enormous weight of the torso, to which that of the rider must be added, has to be carried on few relatively slight supports, a problem already discussed on page 61.

Beginning with the *Gattamelata* we find the ancient skill in representing the horse, to be observed in the *Marcus Aurelius* and the horses of St Mark's, once more regained. Donatello posed his horse on three legs planted on the ground, the fourth, a foreleg, resting on a ball. Verrocchio went further in designing his monument to Bartolomeo Colleone da Bergamo in Venice and raised one foreleg, thus following more closely the pose of the *Marcus Aurelius*. Leonardo da Vinci (1452–1519), Verrocchio's pupil, with greater

Ill. 129

128. Detail of *Ill. 126*. The formidable difficulties in the way of casting such a monument led, in at least one instance, to a painted version being substituted – the *Sir John Hawkwood* of Uccello.

daring raised both forelegs from the ground in a rearing attitude in a model made in stucco for the Sforza monument. This statue of Francesco Sforza appeared in its stucco version at the wedding in Milan of the Emperor Maximilian to Bianca Maria Sforza, where it was placed under a triumphal arch, but it was never cast in bronze, and it is now known only from drawings. Leonardo, in a letter to Lodovico Sforza (Ludovic the Moor) claimed to be able to execute sculpture in marble, bronze, or clay.

Ill. 130

This pose became a favourite in the seventeenth and eighteenth centuries, the weight being carefully balanced on the two hind legs and a heavy tail. Of this category a statue of Philip IV of Spain at Madrid by Pietro Tacca (1577–1640) is an example, and a reduction of the horse without the rider is in the Palazzo Venezia in Rome. The most famous of all is the giant statue of Peter the Great in Leningrad, done by Falconet in 1766.

129. The monument to the *condottiere*, Bartolommeo Colleone, by Andrea Verrocchio, and cast after his death by Alessandro Leopardi. It gives a greater sense of movement than the more classically based *Gattamelata* of Donatello.

130. Leonardo da Vinci. Design for an equestrian statue. Sforza Monument. Three bronze horses are known based on Leonardo's designs, probably cast from wax models made as an aid to his fresco depicting the Battle of Anghiari, *c.* 1508.

In the *Gattamelata* Donatello did more than revive the practice of equestrian statuary. The head of Erasmo is a splendid example of portraiture unmatched since Roman days, and because of this the man is not, as in most such works, dominated by the horse. In this monument Donatello took up afresh a problem which had been neglected for more than a thousand years, and his solution is fully in the spirit of Classical times.

Donatello's first work after his arrival in Padua, where he appears to have established a workshop on a large scale, was a bronze Christ to be placed on a wooden cross. This was followed by a commission for a High Altar for the Basilica of St Anthony which occupied the

131. *Putto* with a fish. Donatello's workshop. *c.* 1455. Originally part of a wall-fountain. Moulds, and wax and *stucco* figures, accumulated in every workshop, to be used as required either by the master himself or by his assistants.

three years from 1447 to 1450. The altar was destroyed *c.* 1580, but the sculptures were preserved. No record now survives of its original appearance although attempts have been made to reconstruct it. For this altar Donatello executed numerous works in bronze, a Madonna and Child, several statues of saints, and four relief panels depicting the Miracles of St Anthony which mark yet another stage in the development of his art.

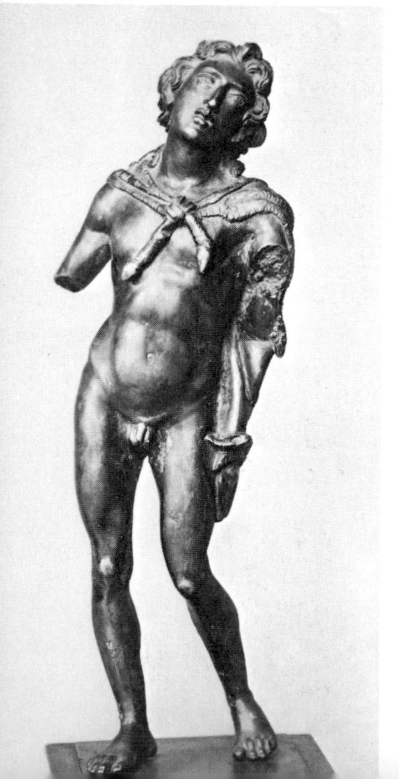

132. Francesco di Giorgio Martini (1439–1502). *Young Bacchante*. So great was the enthusiasm for the antique that small contemporary bronzes were modelled to imitate the damaged condition in which the old ones were excavated.

It was also about this time that the fashion for collecting small bronzes is first to be observed and, stimulated by the excavation of Roman bronzes of this kind by eager antiquarians, they greatly increased in favour towards the end of the fifteenth century. No doubt Donatello's workshop found them profitable, and they soon progressed from mere copies of the antique to being works of art in their own right. They appear first in Padua, then in Venice, and they were being produced in Florence in the days of Lorenzo de' Medici.

Perhaps to be numbered among the pupils of Donatello was Andrea del Verrocchio (1435–88) whose *Incredulity of St Thomas* for the Guild of Merchants was placed in a niche by Donatello at Orsanmichele in 1488. His best-known work is the Colleone monument at Venice which was completed by Alessandro Leopardi after his death. A bronze *David* cast in 1476 and now in the Bargello is the first instance of the kind of face better known from the paintings of Leonardo da Vinci, whose master he was. Another Florentine workshop influenced by Donatello was that of Antonio Pollaiuolo

Ill. 133

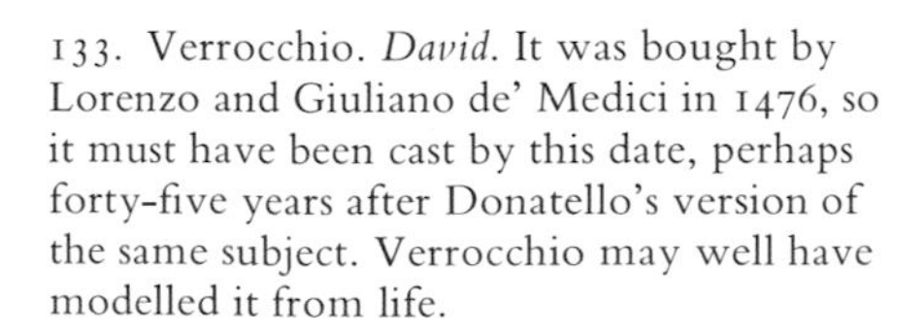

133. Verrocchio. *David*. It was bought by Lorenzo and Giuliano de' Medici in 1476, so it must have been cast by this date, perhaps forty-five years after Donatello's version of the same subject. Verrocchio may well have modelled it from life.

(1433–98) and his brother Piero, who were painters, sculptors, engravers, and goldsmiths and the first to practise the technique of oil-painting. They were also among the first to study the problems presented by the representation of violent action. Bertholdo da Giovanni, another pupil of Donatello's, provides a link between his master and Michelangelo, since it was to Bertholdo that the young Michelangelo was apprenticed.

Ill. 134

One of the most prolific makers of small bronzes at the end of the fifteenth century was the Paduan Andrea Briosco, whose hair

134. Bertholdo da Giovanni was Donatello's pupil and, for a year, master of Michelangelo. Apparently a prolific bronzeworker little is known of him, and Bode first noted the characteristics of his style in 1908. This bronze of Bellerophon struggling with the winged Pegasus is typical of a number of studies of vigorous action ascribed to him.

135, 136. A pair of female grotesques with webbed feet and dolphin tail. *Cf.* Montaigne '. . . Ends in a fish for parts inferior.' Sixteenth century.

gained him the nickname of Riccio (curly). Riccio was born in 1470, the son of a Milanese goldsmith, and his work includes bronzes based on *grotesques* which were taken from frescoes in the newly-discovered Golden House of Nero engraved and published in 1507. This discovery was to have a profound effect on Renaissance decoration, and these essentially Roman motifs form an essential part of the grammar of Renaissance ornament, which received no substantial additions until the discovery of Herculaneum and Pompeii in the eighteenth century. Montaigne refers to these 'antike workes, and monstrous bodies, patched and hudled up together of divers members, without any certaine or well-ordered figure, having neither order, dependencie, or proportion', and quotes Horace:

> A woman fair for parts superior,
> Ends in a fish for parts inferior.

139. Riccio. A lamp in the form of a grotesque monster. Early sixteenth century.

137 (*far left*). *Satyr*. From the workshop of Riccio. First half of the sixteenth century. The fashion for grotesques provided inspiration for the makers of small bronzes, and this lively model belongs to this category. *Cf. Ill. 56*.

138 (*left*). Riccio. *Boy struggling with a goose*. Small bronze figures such as this probably became fashionable in Padua before they were popular elsewhere. A large version, inspired by this one, occurs as a fountain in Basel.

140 (*right*). Riccio. *Mounted Warrior*. This seems undoubtedly to be the first of several known examples, and certainly the finest. One in Germany lacks the helmet, and one in America has the head bending forward to look at a snake under the horse's fore-hoofs.

The bronzeworkers employed these figures terminating either in animal or plant forms in great profusion, and it is evident from his work that Riccio had studied the engravings, since he made statuettes, ornamental oil-lamps, door-knockers, fire-dogs, ink-stands, and many other small and decorative objects in this form, or influenced by it. *Ills. 137–9*

But Riccio did not confine himself to *grotesques*. An exceptionally fine example of his skill is shown here. This model exists in several versions, of which the one shown is the best and probably the earliest. Small divergencies among surviving examples, however, suggest that Riccio's workshop had developed a system of dividing *Ill. 140* the figure into parts, moulding each part separately and making wax casts which were joined together for casting in bronze. This is an ancient technique to be found among the pottery figure-makers of Tanagra before the present era, and an assumption of this kind not only accounts for the observed discrepancies between one version and another, but it facilitated the introduction of variations and modifications for which a new prototype would otherwise have had to be made.

Michelangelo (1474–1564) in this context is much more important for his influence on the subsequent course of Italian sculpture than for his bronzes. He made a bronze *David* for Florence, and a roundel for some Flemish merchants. Both have disappeared, and the second may not even have been cast. Michelangelo was also commissioned to make a bronze portrait statue of Pope Julius II which was fifteen feet in height. It was cast with the aid of a cannon-founder, Maestro Bernardino d'Antonio, and the head alone weighed six hundred pounds. This was melted for cannon in 1511, and, parenthetically, it is pertinent to record the advice of Alberti that bronzes should be cast of a thickness no greater than a knife's edge so that they could not later tempt the cannon-founder with a mass of metal. No designs for the statue of Julius appear to exist, but contemporary records suggest that 17,500 pounds of bronze were employed to cast it. Although nothing by Michelangelo in bronze survives, his letters refer to some of the numerous problems of casting.

Of two bronzeworkers intimately connected with Michelangelo the first, Pietro Torregiano (1472–1528), has perhaps achieved the greater fame as the man who broke Michelangelo's nose. He, also, was one of Bertholdo's pupils, and he fascinated Cellini, who writes that he had the air rather of a great soldier than of a sculptor – 'his frown was enough to scare the bravest'. He continues: 'And every day he would tell us of ruffling it with those beasts of Englishmen.' The last refers to Torregiano's period in England, when he was engaged on the tomb of Henry VII at Westminster.

Benvenuto Cellini (1500–71), the greatest of the Renaissance metalworkers, was much admired by Michelangelo who, after the casting of the great *Perseus* at Florence, wrote: 'My Benvenuto, I

141. Riccio (Andrea Briosco) established his reputation with this bronze candelabrum – the great Paschal Candlestick from the Basilica of San Antonio of Padua. The decoration is Classical in inspiration and full of largely obscure allegory with which he has freely mingled Christian motifs.

142. The Loggia dei Lanzi in Florence (so called because in the days of Cosimo I it was guarded by German lancers) was designed for semi-public ceremonies and richly furnished with sculpture, of which Cellini's *Perseus* (1554) is the most dramatic. The decoration of the pedestal is also his work.

143. *The Head of Medusa.* Sketch model by Cellini as a preliminary study for the *Perseus*. There is some divergence from the final form. Cellini describes the casting of this work in his autobiography.

have long known you to be the best goldsmith in the world; now I know you to be an equally good sculptor.' Symonds wrote of Cellini's *Memoirs*: 'the Genius of the Renaissance incarnate in a single person leans forth and speaks to us', and they give us a fascinating picture of a swashbuckling adventurer who was also master of his art. Cellini's treatise on goldsmiths' work is as essential to the study of the metalworking arts of the sixteenth century as the *De Diversis Artibus* of Theophilus is to the medieval period. Few of Cellini's works either as a sculptor or a goldsmith have survived. Most have suffered the fate of so much of the metalwork of the past – they have been melted for cannon or coin.

The phase we call the High Renaissance becomes more or less apparent both in Florence and Rome shortly before 1500. It was a time of passionate interest in the principles underlying Classical art and architecture, as well as of new departures from Classical tradition. Representations of the nude figures, especially those of Michelangelo who was universally accepted as the greatest painter of his day, began to have a marked effect on the course of Italian painting and sculpture.

Ancient Greek architecture and sculpture were both governed to a considerable degree by the Greek passion for mathematics and geometry, and complex theories of ideal proportion to which works of art were expected to conform were worked out. These rules reached Renaissance man by way of Roman writers. Pliny refers to them briefly, but they were discussed in much greater detail by Vitruvius, who probably took them from the writings of a Greek named Pamphilus, and they were eagerly discussed and adopted not only by many of the architects of the day but by sculptors and painters. Dürer published a treatise on the subject in 1528, and Vitruvian man is the subject of a well known drawing by Leonardo, who represents him as described in Book III, Chapter I of the *Ten Books of Architecture*, with legs and arms extended to form an X contained within a circle which has the navel as its centre. The entire body was divided into two halves at the pubic bone, and it was further subdivided with the head as the unit of measurement. These

144. Bust of Cosimo I (1519–74) by Cellini. Cosimo, Cellini's patron, was a descendant of Lorenzo de' Medici, and was created Grand Duke of Tuscany in 1570.

145. Cellini's version of the Mannerist style is well shown in his *Ganymede mounted on Zeus* who is in the form of an eagle. His skill as a craftsman in metal remains unsurpassed.

proportions were considered to have an ideal significance, and Vitruvius links them with architecture in saying 'that since nature has designed the human body so that its members are duly proportioned to the frame as a whole, it appears that the ancients had good reasons for their rule, that in perfect buildings the different members must be in exact symmetrical relationship'.

Conforming to mathematically-based rules, however, limited freedom of expression, and beginning with Michelangelo, a new approach to Classical tradition is to be observed which culminated in the Mannerist style, current in Italy from *c.* 1520 to the end of the sixteenth century. Mannerist sculptors modelled the human figure in strained and often distorted poses (to which such subjects as

146. Antonio Pollaiuolo. *Hercules and Anteus*. Pollaiuolo was one of the first to study the human figure in violent action, and his *Battle of the Nude Men* (1470) is probably the best known of his many drawings of the subject. This bronze is perhaps the finest version of a very popular Renaissance theme.

147. *Hercules and the Nemean Lion*. Florentine. Early sixteenth century. The Labours of Hercules were always a favourite theme with Renaissance bronze-workers. This one occurs in several versions, and the group is sometimes called *David and the Lion* in reference to the somewhat similar story told in I Samuel XVII.

148. *The Rape of the Sabine*, a marble of 1579–83 by Gian da Bologna in the Loggia dei Lanzi which links the Mannerist and Baroque styles. It is more familiar from bronze reductions, the earliest and best no doubt from Gian's workshop.

Hercules and Anteus or the Rape of the Sabines were especially appropriate), and surface anatomical details were emphasized. The figure, also, was often elongated in defiance of Classical theories of proportion. The purpose was to add to the dramatic effect of the work, and to heighten its emotional content. Cellini, much under the influence of Michelangelo in his later work, belonged to the Mannerist school. So, too, did the influential and prolific maker of small bronzes, Giovanni da Bologna (1529–1608), who was born Jean Boulogne at Douai. Most of his working life was passed in Florence, where he attracted the attention of Francesco de' Medici, and the most outstanding of his works in the Mannerist convention is undoubtedly *The Rape of the Sabine*, 1579–83, a marble which has been the subject of innumerable bronze reductions, some of them *Ill. 148* perhaps almost contemporary. This work was intended to be of equal interest from any angle of view, and it influenced the subsequent course of Florentine sculpture. It is, perhaps, hardly as well known as his *Mercury* of 1564 which has been the subject of innumerable reductions, a few from his own workshop but most as late as the nineteenth century.

Ill. 151

Bronze was more suited than marble to the Mannerist style because of the greater technical freedom which the medium permitted. Cellini's *Perseus* and Gian da Bologna's *Mercury* are examples of poses which are impossible in stone, and if a design proved to be too elaborate for casting in one piece, it could always be cast in sections and welded together afterwards.

Gian maintained a workshop for the making of small decorative bronzes designed by him, by his pupils, and his assistants. Examples

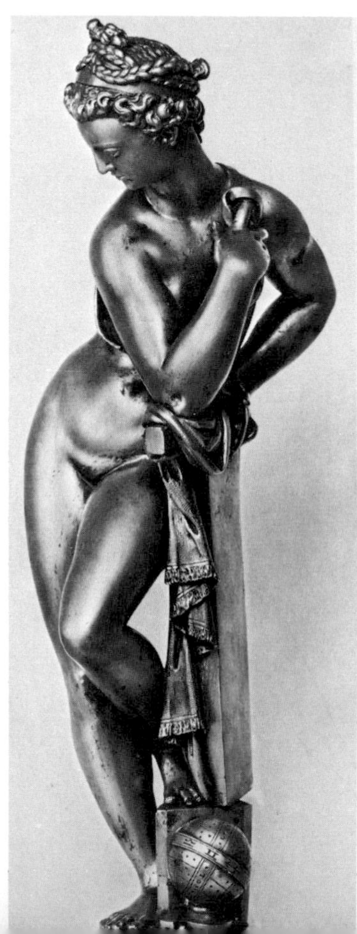

are fairly numerous today, and most deserve no closer attribution than 'School of Giovanni da Bologna'. Some are direct copies of antique works, which continued to be popular, some were adapted from this source, and others were original designs or reductions of large works. The numbers surviving testify to their popularity at the time.

The best known of Gian's pupils, Pietro Tacca, was noted for his skill in modelling animals. The famous bronze *Boar*, after the antique, in Florence is from his hand, and it was he who completed his master's equestrian statue of Henri Quatre which stood in the middle of the Pont-Neuf in Paris until the Revolution. Evelyn, who saw it in 1643, said that 'it exceeds the natural proportions by much'. Another pupil, Antonio Susini, was a prolific maker of small bronzes. Yet another pupil, the Flemish Adriaen de Vries (1546–1626),

149 (*far left*). Allegory was a favourite Renaissance theme which persisted well into the eighteenth century. This symbolizes *Virtue triumphing over Vice*, one of several versions of this subject. After Gian da Bologna. Second half of the sixteenth century.

150 (*left*). Gian da Bologna. *Astronomy*. Gilded bronze. It clearly shows the Mannerist habit of twisting the parts of the body into different directions which yet achieve a final balance (*contrapposto*). First to be seen in the works of Donatello, this characteristic became much exaggerated in the sixteenth century.

151 (*right*). Gian da Bologna devoted himself almost entirely to mythological subjects. His *Mercury* of 1580 is a development of the Mannerist style. Only bronze could give such freedom to the sculptor.

became Court Sculptor to the Emperor Rudolf II whose portrait bust is in the Victoria and Albert Museum. De Vries was especially active in disseminating the Mannerist style in Austria and southern Germany, and one of his most notable surviving works is the Hercules fountain at Augsburg.

Ill. 153

Space is insufficient to mention many of the makers of what the French call *bronzes d'ameublement* – the furnishing bronzes which decorated Renaissance interiors, but Venice, which maintained a flourishing school of bronzeworkers, to which in medieval times both Greek and German craftsmen contributed, is the source of some of them. The Renaissance came to Venice (the principal *entrepôt* of Italian trade with the East) fairly late in the fifteenth century by way of Padua. The Gothic style lingered in Venice for longer than it did elsewhere in Italy. Verrocchio's monument to Colleone was completed by Leopardi (d. 1522), who was especially skilled as a bronze-caster. The clay or stucco original had reached the stage of completion before the commission was given to Leopardi, but his own work, such as the bronze bases for the standard masts opposite St Mark's, is of excellent workmanship. Andrea Sansovino

152 (*left*). Leone Lione (*c.* 1509–90), goldsmith, medallist, sculptor, and bronzecaster, was Cellini's rival. In the service of the Emperor, he became known as 'Il Scultore Cesareo' from the number of portraits he made of the Imperial family. The illustration is of one of his busts of Charles V.

153 (*right*). Adriaen de Vries. The Mercury fountain in the Maximilians-strasse at Augsburg, erected in 1599. The sculptor's debt to Gian da Bologna, whose pupil he was, is easily perceptible.

STELLTEN

(1460–1529) was a Florentine who studied under Pollaiuolo and Bertholdo, and he was the master of Jacopo Tatti (1486–1570) who adopted his name and became known as Jacopo Sansovino. The two men visited Rome together, and Jacopo then turned to antique sculpture as a source of inspiration. He is generally regarded as the most influential Venetian sculptor of the High Renaissance, and several bronze statues from his hand have survived, as well as the doors of the Sacristy of St Mark's. Perhaps his finest bronze is the *Hermes* of the Logetta. Alessandro Vittoria (1525–1608) was one of Jacopo's assistants who was more strongly influenced by Michelangelo than by his master. In addition to his larger works some excellent small bronzes have been attributed to his hand. Another of Jacopo's assistants, Danese Cattaneo (1509–73), also made small bronzes, as did Cattaneo's own pupil, Girolamo Campagna (1549–*c.* 1626). Tiziano Aspetti (1565–1607) was one of Vittoria's followers whose small bronzes are sought. His *Minerva* was the subject of a

Ill. 154

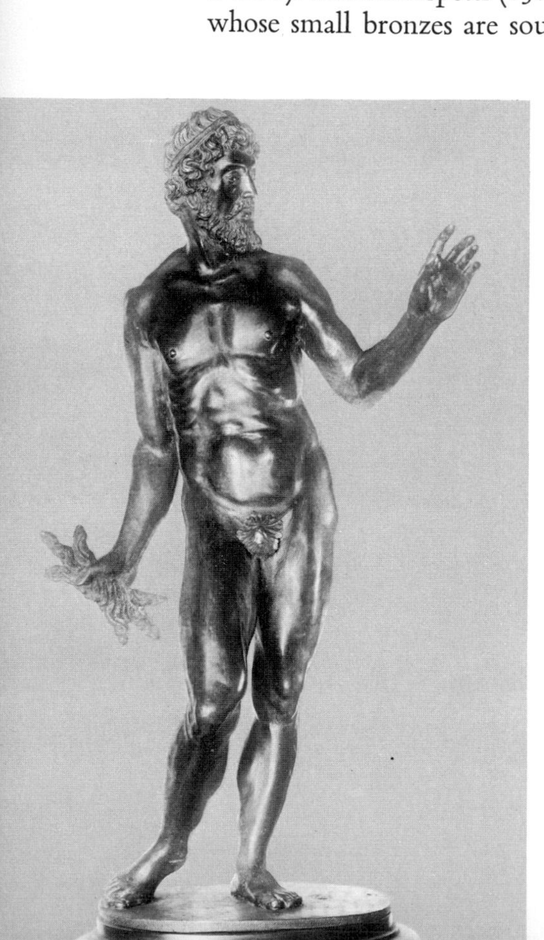

154. *Jupiter* by Jacopo Tatti, called Sansovino (1486–1570). Sculptor, architect, restorer of ancient statuary, and bronzecaster, Sansovino was a fine craftsman who, while in Rome, cast a bronze copy of the Laocoön.

clever forgery by the Viennese bronzeworker and enameller, Solomon Weininger, in the 1870s. Forgeries of small bronzes, both ancient and of the Renaissance, are not unknown, and some Renaissance bronzes themselves began their existence as forgeries of old Roman work. When, as in the case of Aspetti's *Minerva*, they are cast from moulds taken from an original, forgeries can often be difficult to detect, especially when we remember that minor variations in several genuine versions of the same bronze often exist.

Small bronzes from Rome which can be dated before the beginning of the seventeenth century are rare. The arts had been neglected in the Eternal City from the ninth century to the fifteenth, and had then revived with the accession of Pope Julius II (1443–1513), perhaps the most influential of all the Papal patrons of the arts.

Little bronze sculpture was made in fifteenth-century France. Most of the available metal was going to make larger and more efficient cannon which were an essential part of French military equipment. The Italian Wars of the early years of the sixteenth century brought the Renaissance to France, and the revived Classical styles made their *début* at Fontainebleau, whither the King invited Italian artists and craftsmen of all kinds. By 1526 the Gothic style was rapidly being abandoned for secular purposes, and as the century unfolded there is to be seen an increasing richness and variety in manufactures of all kinds, including works in bronze. Cellini, in his *Memoirs*, testifies to the French skill in the casting of large quantities of bronze at this time.

The Mannerist Francesco Primaticcio (1504–70) was entrusted with the decoration of Fontainebleau by François Premier in 1542, and in 1559 he became the principal decorative artist to Catherine de' Medici with a workshop in Paris. Primaticcio – painter, sculptor, and architect – journeyed to Rome to bring back replicas of ancient statuary for the royal palace, and took moulds of those things which he was unable to carry off. Among them was the equestrian statue of Marcus Aurelius which, cast in plaster, was set up in the Cour de Cheval Blanc. The Court records refer to sums paid to Jean le Roux, called Picart, who was charged with the casting of Michelangelo's *Pietà*, and some of Primaticcio's moulds were employed to take bronze casts. These, and the statues he brought back to France, were seen by Evelyn when he visited Fontainebleau in 1644. Evelyn refers to a *Mercury*, a 'Diana ejecting a fountain', a 'fountain of Tyber of a Colossean figure of Brass', and a 'Wolf over Romulus and Remus' – the Capitoline wolf.

Cellini was first in France in 1537. His second visit began in 1540 and he stayed until 1543, doing the well known *Nymph of Fontainebleau* for the King in that year. He also designed a figure of Mars intended to represent François surrounded by figures symbolizing the arts, sciences, and philosophy. Primaticcio, in favour with the King's mistress, secured the commission instead.

Ill. 156

No doubt the technical knowledge which Cellini brought with him influenced the art of bronze-casting in France, but the stylistic influence was Primaticcio's. This is evident from the work of Germain Pilon (1535–90) who, with Jean Goujon, dominated the second half of the century. Both were strongly influenced by Italy. Goujon, a Huguenot, probably fled from France about the year 1563 to escape persecution. Pilon knew both Primaticcio, and Philibert de l'Orme, who built the Château of Anet for Diane de Poitiers. He

Ill. 155

155. *Charles IX* of France by Germaine Pilon (1537–90). Pilon was much influenced by Primaticcio and the Italians of Fontainebleau. Of his religious sculpture, there is a bronze pictorial relief of the Deposition in the Louvre.

156. *The Nymph of Fontainebleau* of 1543, executed by Cellini for François Premier but taken by Diane de Poitiers, future mistress of Henri Deux, for the gateway of her château at Anet. It is now in the Louvre.

was attracted to the nude figure as a Renaissance revival of the antique mode, and his bronze relief of *The Deposition* in the Louvre, in which the influence of Michelangelo is perceptible, is pictorial in its conception.

The Renaissance is first to be seen in Germany soon after 1500, and by this year a prosperous metal industry had been established in southern Germany. Its richest and most influential banker, Hans Fugger of Augsburg, was financing and exploiting copper-mines in Hungary and the Tyrol, in which he had the assistance and support of the Emperor Maximilian, the 'Last Knight'. The founding of the House of Fugger as a corporation, the first of its kind on German soil, dates from 1494, and the Fuggers were among the most influential of Europe's art-patrons at the time.

For many years south Germany had supported a flourishing school of woodcarving, the two most important names being Veit

Stoss (fl. 1475–1533) and Tilman Riemenschneider (?1468–1531). Both worked in a late Gothic style. The greatest single factor in disseminating the novel styles of the Renaissance in south Germany was undoubtedly the print, for which engraved copper plates provided an alternative to the wood-block. The engraving of copper plates was not new. They are to be found in the form of commemorative brasses, and smaller plates of the kind were affixed to wooden foundations in the making of reliquaries. According to Vasari the inventor of engraving for the special purpose of printing was a goldsmith named Finiguerra (1426–64), who took impressions as a record of his work, and the subsequent adaptation to the special purpose of printing was greatly extended by Marcantonio Raimondi (1487–1539) who copied the paintings of Raphael and others. Vasari, however, was probably in error in attributing the invention to Finiguerra, and the process may have been in use in Germany before 1446. Apart from Raimondi, Albrecht Dürer (1471–1528) and Lucas van Leyden (1494–1533) were notable engravers who employed this medium.

Engravings influenced the art of sculpture in Germany because many of them illustrated the new fashions in Italy, and they fathered a whole series of design-books for the use of craftsmen which continued to be a popular form of inspiration throughout Western Europe at least until the beginning of the nineteenth century.

From the middle of the fifteenth century German bronze-founders were using the metal in increasing quantities. A bell for Cologne Cathedral weighing eleven tons had been cast in 1448, but one for Erfurt, cast in 1497, weighed fourteen tons. Cannon-founders were also producing ever-larger pieces of ordnance, often highly decorative objects, and an unusually large wine-cistern in the Bayerisches Museum in Munich, about four feet high, of similar diameter, and half an inch thick, was cast by a cannon-founder, Sebald Hirder,

157. The *Sebaldusgrab* at Nürnberg by Peter Vischer and his sons (completed 1519). Although still Gothic in style much of the small sculptural decoration is clearly influenced by Italian models. It is transitional between the dying Gothic and the newly revived Classicism of the Renaissance.

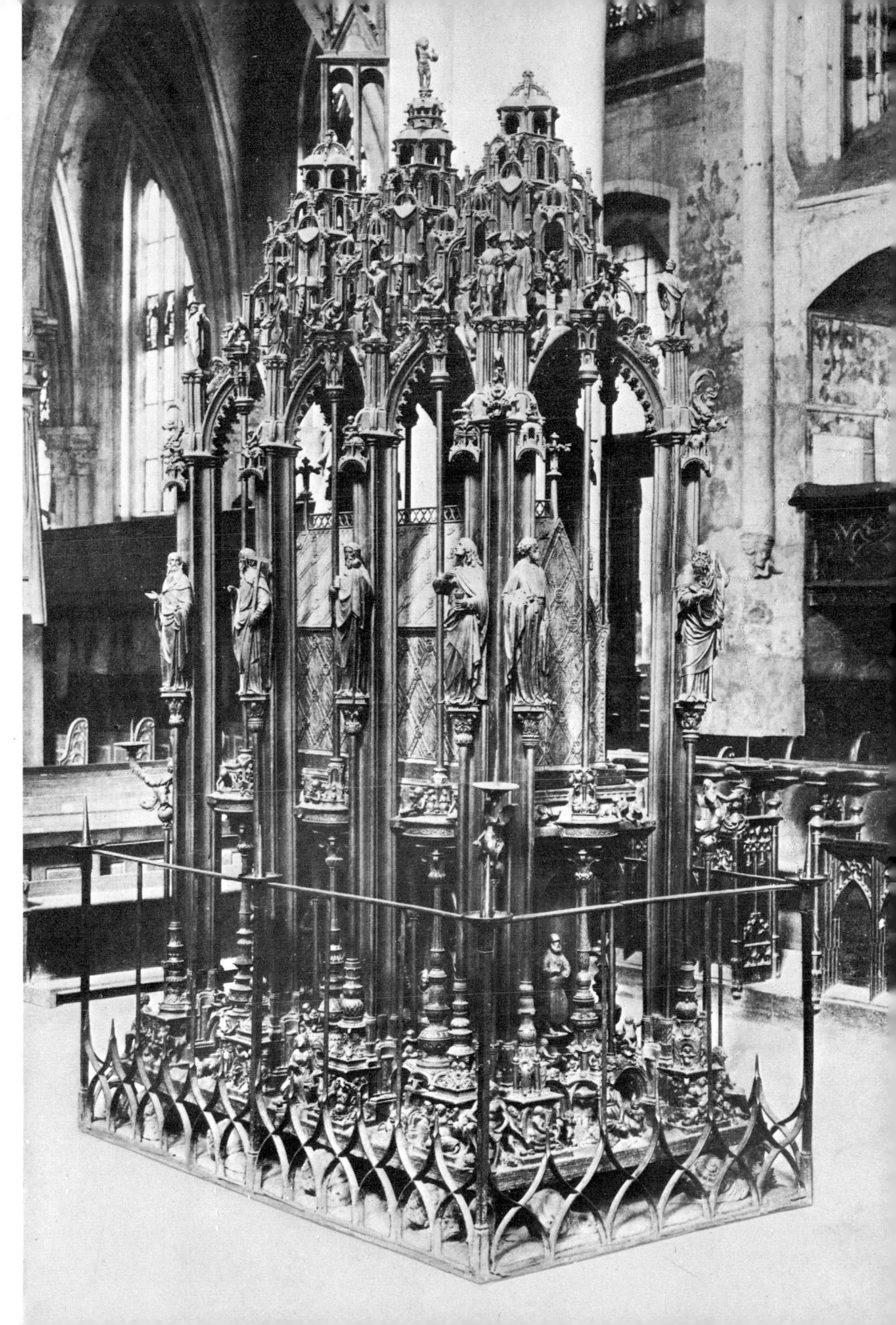

158. Detail of *Ill. 157*. The *Leuchterweiben* – female grotesques supporting pricket candleholders.

159. This lion was originally intended to form part of the base of Peter Vischer's Tomb of Saint Sebald, but snails were finally substituted.

160. Peter Vischer's self-portrait from the *Sebaldusgrab*. The Church of St Sebald, badly damaged during the war, has been magnificently restored.

in 1543. The frieze of vine leaves and grapes which decorates it is in the new style. Later we continue to hear of cannon-founders as casters of bronze statuary, for instance, the eighteenth-century statue of Augustus the Strong in Dresden Neustadt cast by Ludwig Wiedmann.

Peter Vischer is the first of the great German sculptors in bronze whose work can be attributed. It encompassed both the late Gothic and the early revived Classical style. The Classical element might, perhaps, have been even stronger but for the fact that most of his work was done for an ecclesiastical setting which was Gothic in style. Some of it exhibits the least desirable features of Gothic inseparable from the later manifestations of the style, but these were combined with Renaissance motifs of the kind to be observed in

162. The Tomb of the Holy Roman Emperor, Maximilian I (the last Knight) in the Hofkirche, Innsbruck.

the Tomb of St Sebald at Nürnberg, which was his greatest work and a textbook example of the transition between the two styles.

Sebald was an eighth-century saint who converted the heathen Nürnbergers, and Peter and his son worked on this ambitious monument from 1488 to 1519. The sarcophagus itself resembles a *chasse*, or reliquary, set within Gothic arcades and crowned with an *Ills. 157–60*

161. Detail of *Ill. 162.* Three of Maximilian's ancestors. Left, King Arthur of England by Peter Vischer. Representation of ancestors was a fairly well-established custom in northern Europe, although hardly on so lavish a scale.

163. Limewood-carving was the origin of many South German bronzes because the softness of the wood and the lack of a well-marked grain made it especially suitable for the purpose. This is the model for the well-known sixteenth-century Nürnberg fountain, the *Gänsemännchen*, by Pancraz Labenwolf.

164 (*right*). Another view of Maximilian's tomb, one of the finest in northern Europe. Designed by Gilg Sesselschreiber, the Court Painter, the work was a co-operative undertaking which took several generations to complete. Maximilian in bronze kneels on the marble sarcophagus.

elaborate Gothic canopy which has all the fussiness of ornament common to the period. This is supported on the backs of large bronze snails, although the original intention was to use lions instead. There are numerous figures of apostles, prophets, and saints, including Sebald himself, and a portrait of the sculptor, and the occurrence of such Renaissance motifs as *putti* and *grotesques*, the latter in the form of nude, winged, female half-figures terminating in foliage (the *Leuchterweiben* who support pricket candleholders) is perhaps a little incongruous. They occur only a few years after *grotesques* had first become fashionable in Italy, and were no doubt taken from engravings.

Ill. 159

Ill. 160

Ill. 158

Another important tomb of the period, in the making of which Peter Vischer the Elder participated, is that of Maximilian in the Hofkirche at Innsbruck. This was a much more ambitious project than the Sebald tomb and, begun in 1508, it was not completed

Ills. 161–2, 164

until 1582. The general design was by the Augsburg Court Painter, Gilg Sesselschreiber, and the figure of Maximilian, whose body is buried elsewhere, was by Ludovico Scalza, called del Duca.

It was the intention that Maximilian should lie surrounded by effigies of his ancestors, and two of the finest come from the hand of Peter Vischer – King Arthur of England and Theodoric the Ostrogoth. Arthur, recognizably English, wears richly decorated armour and stands with lowered shield which is quartered with lions rampant and the fleur-de-lys. Most of these statues were cast at a bronze-foundry established by Maximilian near Innsbruck, at Mühlau.

Ill. 161

Of the other German bronzeworkers of the period it is essential to mention Peter Vischer the Younger, and his brother Hans. Pancraz Labenwolf is especially worthy of notice. His well known fountain, the *Gänsemännchen*, depicting a man with a goose under either arm, still survives in Nürnberg, but being quite small and protected by an iron grill which partially obscures it is easily overlooked. A more satisfactory representation of this delightful little work is a limewood version carved *c.* 1530 and preserved in the

Ill. 163

165. Part of a table-fountain representing Apollo and Daphne. Peter Flötner. Nürnberg. *c.* 1540.

Germanisches Nationalmuseum. Peter Flötner (*c.* 1485–1546), a Swiss by birth, was working in Nürnberg in 1522. His work suggests a period in Italy, whence several German sculptors went to study, but specimens are rare and most are doubtfully attributed. Konrad Veit of Worms, of whom Dürer said: 'that excellent carver whose equal I have never seen', is represented here by his *Mars and Venus* executed *c.* 1525. Like Vischer, Veit played a large part in promoting the growth of the German Renaissance style, although his work continued to preserve a considerable amount of Gothic realism. It is evident that woodcarving was the first step to many south German bronzes; this is characteristic, and to be seen again later in the limewood prototypes carved by Bustelli for his superb series of porcelain figures at Nymphenburg.

Ill. 165

Ill. 166

Both Augsburg and Nürnberg were notable metalworking centres which commonly used bronze and brass, as well as gilt-bronze. Clocks were marvels of decorative ingenuity, and since many were table-clocks a spring-driven mechanism was essential, an invention somewhat doubtfully attributed to Peter Henlein *c.* 1500.

166. Konrad Veit. *Mars and Venus.* *c.* 1525. The subject is Classical, the treatment still with Gothic overtones. Notice, for instance, the height of Venus, who is shorter than the seated Mars.

167. Limewood model for the handles of a vase in either gold or bronze. Probably Nürnberg, *c.* 1580. This is an excellent example of the later type of grotesque to be seen also in the decoration of Italian *maiolica* soon after 1550. The figure terminates in acanthus foliage.

168. (*right*). *Henry VII and his Consort Elizabeth of York.* The effigy was completed within twenty years of his death by Torregiano.

Small table-fountains and centre-pieces were a speciality of the Augsburg metal-craftsman during the sixteenth and seventeenth centuries, while large garden-fountains were made to order. It was customary to put small fountains together from stock figures, and methods of multiplying casts were developed. It is probable that many surviving figures of uncertain purpose were once part of this kind of ornamental metalwork. In the eighteenth century, according to a contemporary French writer, people sometimes changed the figures adorning their clock-cases for others, and there is no reason to assume that the custom was a particularly new one. Wall-cisterns of bronze are a rare survival from Augsburg.

The Renaissance came a little late to the Low Countries, but the new movement is to be seen both in sculpture and metalwork by the 1530s, brought by minor Italian artists working in Flanders, by imports of contemporary Italian art by way of Antwerp which was a flourishing centre of the art-trade, or as a product of the visits of Flemish artists to Italy, and it continued to gather strength. Sometimes the travellers to Italy did not return, for instance he who became Giovanni da Bologna.

In England the influence of the Renaissance is first perceptible in the Tomb of Henry VII at Westminster which, with its surrounding chapel, caused Bacon to say that Henry 'dwelt more richly dead than he did alive in any of his palaces'. Much of the bronzework is from the hand of the Florentine Pietro Torregiano (called Peter Torrysany in contemporary English records) who was assisted by Humfray Walker and Nicholas Ewen, respectively a bronze-founder and a coppersmith. The doors of bronze plates affixed to a wooden substructure are the only example of work of this kind in England.

Ill. 168

Torregiano was one of the large number of Italian craftsmen of all kinds brought to England, principally by Wolsey, in the reign of Henry VIII, and many worked at Hampton Court and Nonsuch Palace, although most were plasterers and carvers. Torregiano arrived in 1513, and soon gained a remarkable reputation as a sculptor in bronze, marble, and wood. Evidently dissatisfied with the services of Walker and Ewen he returned to Florence to seek more expert help. He tried to recruit Cellini, and but for his assault on Michelangelo, Cellini's friend, the latter might well have added something of note to the history of decorative metalwork in England.

The Tomb of Henry VII, largely Gothic in style, is, like the Sebald tomb, an example of the transitional phase between the old and the new. For the remainder of the century Flemish influence competed with Italian and, in the reign of Elizabeth I, the most notable English sculptor of the day, Nicholas Stone, was trained in Amsterdam by Pieter de Keyser. His account-books do not mention bronze but only wood and 'marbell', but Dallaway testified to his

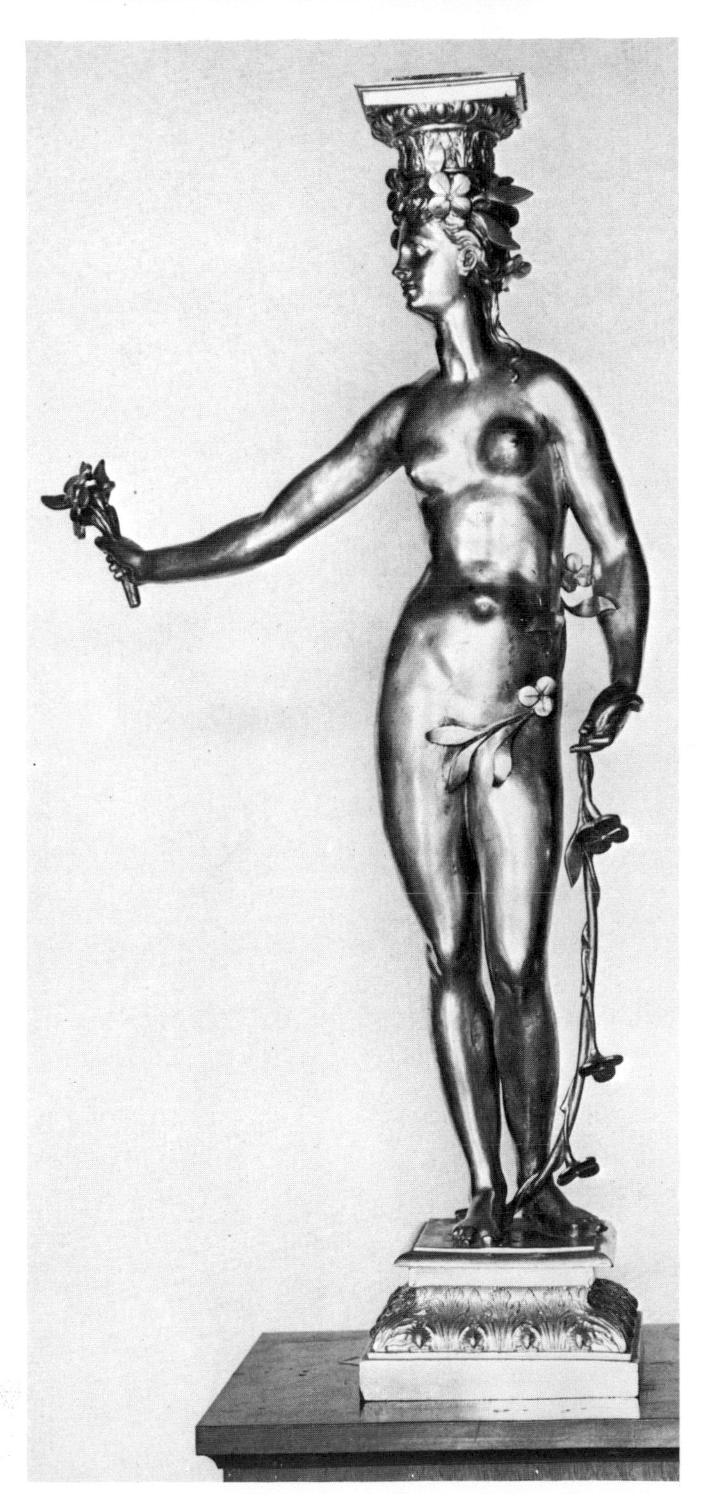

169. *Spring* by Wentzel Jamnitzer and J. G. van der Schardt. Gilded bronze. It is one of four allegorical figures which once formed part of a fountain. The style is related to that of the School of Fontainebleau.

influence during the first decades of the seventeenth century in writing: 'We owe to Nicholas Stone the full praise of having deviated with more success than his immediate predecessors from the stiff and gothic style, yet his approaches towards classic grace were distant. During the time of his practice the French, Flemish, or Italians brought to England sometimes the manner of Gougeon [Goujon] or Pilon, sometimes a debased imitation of John of Bologna, and sometimes the taste of Bernini, but never a pure style nor sound principles.'

Stone, in Rome in 1638, waited on the 'Cav. Bernini'. To him is sometimes attributed the fashion for English portrait statues wearing Roman armour. Very little bronze-casting seems to have been done in England from the departure of Torregiano to the coming of Hubert Le Soeur or Le Sueur, whose work is discussed in the following chapter, in 1630.

170. Pietro Tacca. Inkstand in the form of a monkey taking a baby from its cradle. First quarter of the seventeenth century. An early *bronze d'ameublement*.

CHAPTER SIX

The seventeenth century

'Under the cupola', wrote Evelyn describing his visit to St Peter's, 'stands the high altar . . . lately covered by Pope Urban VIII with that sumptuous canopy of Corinthian brass which heretofore was brought from the Pantheon; it consists of four wreathed columns, partly channeled and encircled with vines, on which hang little *putti* and bees (the Arms of the Barberini), sustaining a baldachin of the same metal. The four columns weigh a hundred and ten thousand pounds, all over richly gilt; this, with pedestals, crown, and statues about it, form a thing of that art, vastness, and magnificence, as is beyond all man's industry has produced of the kind; it is the work of Bernini. . . .'

This *baldacchino* is the major work in bronze of Giovanni Lorenzo Bernini (1598–1680), and although his reputation suffered eclipse in the nineteenth century at the hands of Ruskin, who detested all that he stood for, he has today regained esteem as the greatest and most influential of the Baroque sculptors.

Bernini was the son of a Florentine sculptor whose family moved to Rome in 1605, and he only left the city subsequently to make the journey to Paris at the invitation of Colbert when he submitted designs for additions to the Louvre. These were rejected in favour of those of Perrault which were in a more markedly Classical style.

At an early age Bernini gave evidence of a remarkable versatility, of which Evelyn's *Diary* provides contemporary testimony. His youth was spent during a period when the Jesuits were striving to establish a new form of ecclesiastical art which, by dramatizing the Christian faith, would secure the allegiance of those who might be tempted away from the Roman Church by new and more austere heresies.

Bernini was a stone-cutter by choice, and many of his most important works are in stone, or are bronze casts based on an earlier work in stone. But his influence on the art of sculpture in Western Europe was profound, irrespective of material, and it persisted almost until the neo-Classical revival of the middle years of the eighteenth century. The seventeenth century in particular is dominated by Bernini, and just as Michelangelo was the starting-point of Mannerism, so Bernini may be said to have been the origin of Baroque in interior decoration, although the style was later modified in both France and Germany.

His theatrical experience led him to use techniques more appropriate to the stage, and he blended white and coloured marbles with bronze, stucco, and painting. A marble figure *Truth* flanking the central part of the Tomb of Pope Alexander VII, for instance, is partly covered by bronze drapery. Bernini paid careful attention to lighting, sometimes employing stained-glass windows to throw coloured illumination on his work. An example is to be found in the *Chair of St Peter* in St Peter's where marble, gilt-bronze, and stucco are blended into a vast and soaring dramatic composition. This is, perhaps, his most notable work, the casting of which (by Artusi) began in 1660.

Ill. 172

Ill. 171

The *baldacchino* described by Evelyn was an earlier work which is almost entirely of bronze. Bernini received the commission for it in 1624, and it is therefore one of the first of his works to be regarded as truly Baroque. Among his assistants was François Duquesnoy (1594–1643) known as Il Fiammingo from his birthplace in Brussels, and much of the bronze came from the old Roman Pantheon which was despoiled for the purpose.

Bernini excelled in the rendering of intense emotion, which was in keeping with his own character, and the facial expressions of his figures are of a kind not hitherto attempted. This can well be seen in the face of his marble *St Teresa*, where he had portrayed erotic ecstasy thinly disguised as the climax of a mystical experience, and

171. The *Baldacchino* of Bernini in St Peter's, Rome. It is ninety-five feet in height, with a weight of ninety-three tons. It covers the High Altar, and is sited over the Tomb of St Peter.

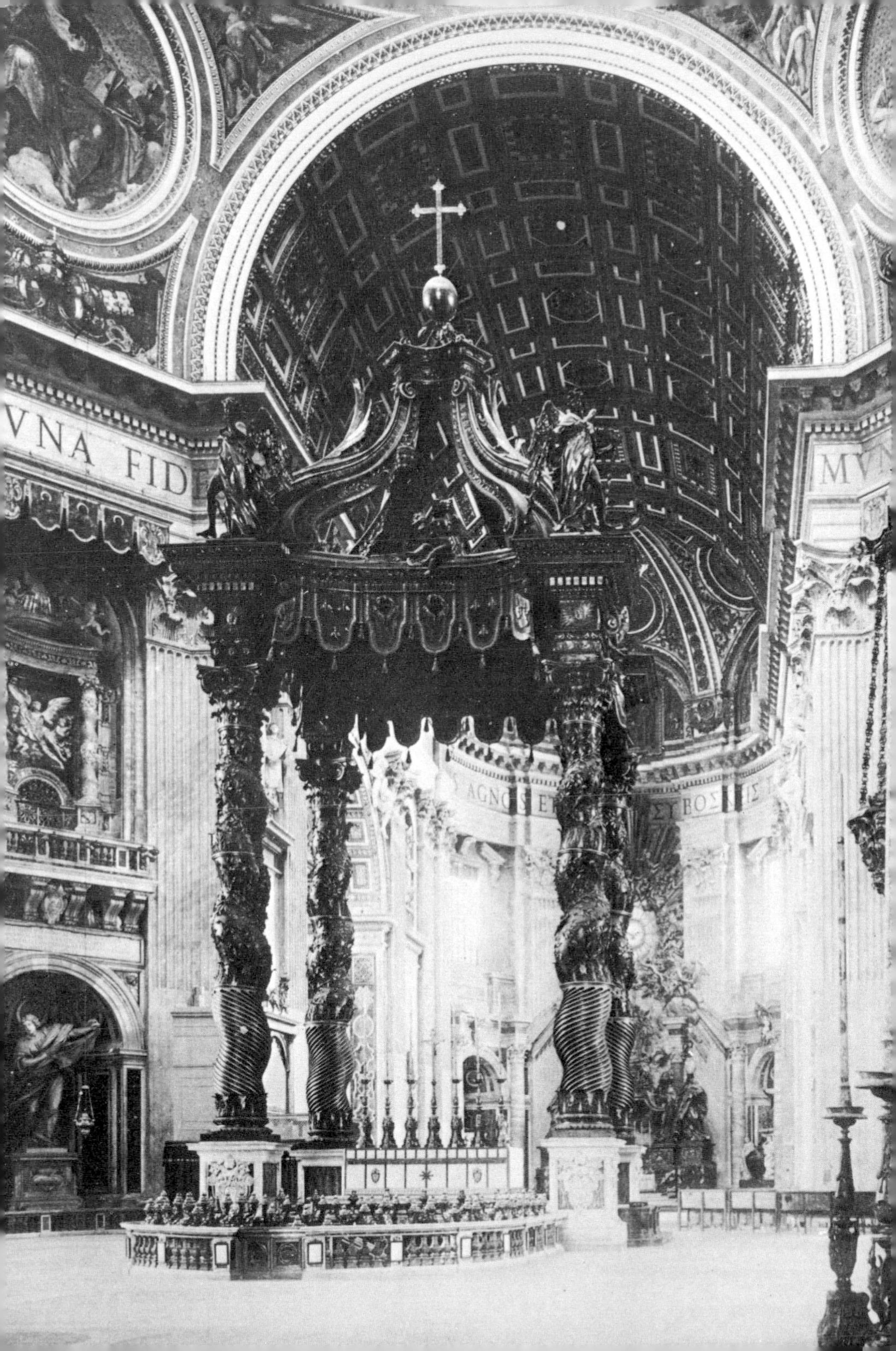
VNA FID

172. Giovanni Lorenzo Bernini. The tomb of Pope Alexander VII, St. Peter's, Rome. In white and coloured marble, and bronze, it is an example of Bernini's use of mixed materials.

173. *Pope Innocent X*. Bronze by Alessandro Algardi (1595–1654). Intended as a counterpart to Urban VIII by Bernini, it is less dramatic as a composition, with less force. Most of Algardi's work was a compromise between the Baroque style and the more severe Classicism inherited from Raphael.

his angels are usually far from the sexless creatures in which form they were customarily represented.

Bernini was also an accomplished portrait sculptor. His portrait marbles are generally finer than his bronzes, and many are in poses more appropriate to bronze. Bernini exhibited an almost unprecedented technical dexterity in his arrangement of massive free-floating parts, which are always carefully calculated to appear an unobtrusive and integral part of the whole composition.

Bernini began as a sculptor in the Classical tradition, and his first known work was so markedly Classical in style that it was at one time regarded as Hellenistic, but he soon turned to the Mannerist convention. From this he had departed by 1624 when he carved his *Apollo and Daphne* in the Galleria Borghese in Rome. His contemporary, Alessandro Algardi (1602–54), was both an enemy and a rival, who worked in the more conventional Classical tradition, although he was by no means uninfluenced by Bernini. The two men represent the two principal streams of influence to be observed during the seventeenth century, the Classicism of Algardi being especially noticeable in French decorative art and the influence of Bernini in the Baroque decorations of southern Germany. Bernini's sculpture has been well described as rhetoric in stone, and some of his large works in marble also occur in the form of bronze reductions. They lose far less from the translation from one medium to another than they do by the reduction in size.

François Duquesnoy, who mainly adhered to the Classical tradition, lived in Italy from 1620 until his death. His style, in fact, was almost always more French than Italian, and his little bronzes of *putti* continued to be imitated until well into the eighteenth century. His best-known bronze is the much-reproduced fountain at Brussels known as the 'manneken-pis'.

By the middle of the century the centre of gravity in European art was shifting to Paris, a process greatly accelerated by the foundation of the Manufacture royale des Meubles de la Couronne by Colbert for the purpose of producing works of art to furnish Versailles and other of the King's palaces. Many Italian bronzeworkers made their way to Paris, some invited by the Italian Cardinal Mazarin.

Versailles was intended to surpass even the palaces of Italy, which it did very successfully, and many of the finest French sculptors of the day were employed to decorate the château and its superb gardens which were laid out by André Le Nôtre. Among them there is space to select only one or two, but Antoine Coysevox (1640–1720), born in Lyon, was one of the most prominent. He was appointed Sculpteur du Roi in 1666, and thereafter was principally employed decorating the various royal châteaux – Versailles, Trianon, Marly, and Saint-Cloud. He executed a number of portraits of Louis Quatorze.

Much of the statuary of the time was cast by the Brothers Keller, cannon-founders at the Paris Arsenal. They were the founders of the *Crouching Venus* of Coysevox, after the antique, and of most of the bronze statues for the Parterre d'Eau at Versailles, which formed one of the most remarkable assemblages of statuary bronzes in Europe. The bronze used by the Kellers was analysed in 1817 by Lemot, who found that it contained 91·1 per cent of copper, 1·7 per cent of tin, 5·53 per cent of zinc, and 1·37 per cent of lead.

François Girardon (1628–1715) was the rival of Coysevox. His work is comparable in quality and often similar in style. His equestrian statue of Louis Quatorze to the design of Hardouin-Mansard was destroyed during the Revolution, but it survives as a reduction. *Ill. 174*

174. *Louis Quatorze* by Girardon. A reduction (height $17\frac{1}{4}$ inches) of the statue described by Martin Lister. Set up in 1699, the original was destroyed during the Revolution in 1792.

Dr Martin Lister, Queen Anne's physician, who left a journal of his visit to Paris in 1698, discussed its making with Girardon. 'This Colossus of Brass is yet in the very place [Place Vendôme] where it was cast; it is surprisingly great, being 22 foot high, the Foot of the King 26 inches in length, and all the proportions of him and the Horse suitable. There was a 100,000 pounds weight of Mettal melted, but it took not above 80,000 pounds [about 35 tons]; it was all cast at once, Horse and Man. Mons. Girardon told me he wrought diligently, and with almost daily application at the Model 8 years, and there were two years more spent in the Moulding, and Furnaces, and Casting of it. The King is in the Habit of a Roman Emperor, without Stirrups or Saddle, and on his Head a French large Periwig à-la-mode. Whence this great Liberty of Sculpture arises I am much to seek.' That Paris craftsmen were not without experience in casting work of this magnitude may be seen from what Cellini had to say about them in 1568: 'I have seen 100,000 lbs. of metal cast at one time with so much ease that I marvelled at it, so great was the technical skill with which it was done. . . .'

Ill. 175 Elsewhere Lister refers to his visit to Versailles where he saw 'a large Basin of Water in the middle [of the Parterres], walled round with white marble, on which are placed a great number of incomparable Brazen Vasa, and large Brass figures couchant of the best Masters in Sculpture'.

Pierre Puget (1620–94) was, perhaps, the only strictly Baroque sculptor working in France during the seventeenth century, and his work was influenced by that of Bernini. He was originally commissioned to make the statues for the gardens of Vaux-le-Vicomte for the Minister Fouquet, but the latter's fall prevented their execution. His masterpiece is the *Milo of Croton* now in the Louvre.

The economic troubles which beset the closing decades of the seventeenth century in France caused Louis Quatorze to send most of his silver furniture to the Mint, and their place was taken by carved wood and gilt-bronze. This period saw the start of the vogue for gilt-bronze as a material for interior decoration, and the influence of the metalworker on furniture design, which was to continue into the eighteenth century and beyond. An Italian, Domenico Cucci,

175. One of a pair of vases by Girardon, the cover missing. This is a reduced contemporary version of large marble vases once in the gardens of Versailles which Girardon made for Colbert. Lister refers to 'Brazen Vasa' at Versailles in 1698.

had already been responsible for framing the mirrors of the Galerie des Glaces in bronze, and André-Charles Boulle (1642–1732), who was both an *ébéniste* and a bronzeworker, developed his characteristic furniture decorated with a marquetry of brass and tortoiseshell, with handsome gilt-bronze mounts, from fashions introduced earlier in the century from Italy and the Low Countries. The mounting of furniture in this way, which has continued to characterize most of the best French furniture since that date, was a revival of an old Roman practice, which was itself ancient in the days of Imperial Rome.

Some of the *ébénistes* working during the early years of the eighteenth century had premises assigned to them in the Paris Arsenal, where the Brothers Keller had earlier cast some of the Versailles statuary, and it was here no doubt that many furniture-mounts were cast. The bronze-casters formed a separate guild – the *fondeurs-ciseleurs*, the reference to chisellers recording the great part they played in finishing the casts. Bronzework in relation to furniture, however, played a much greater part in the eighteenth century, and it is considered in greater detail later.

The seventeenth century also saw the beginning of the vogue for elaborate bronze clock-cases decorated with figures, which reached its highest point during the eighteenth century.

A French sculptor working in England at the beginning of the century was the Huguenot refugee, Hubert Le Sueur, who is sometimes said to have been a pupil of Gian da Bologna. The most that can be said, however, is that he is known to have helped Tacca to finish the equestrian statue of Henri Quatre for the Pont-Neuf after Gian's death, and he studied under the French sculptor Pierre Biard (1559–1609), whose own work was much influenced by the Italians.

Ill. 176

Born in 1595, Le Sueur arrived in England in 1630, and soon after his arrival he was commissioned to make the fine equestrian figure of Charles I at Charing Cross, London's best public statue. Le Sueur received his commission from Lord Treasurer Weston; the agreement has some general interest and part of it is here quoted: '.... an agreement with one Hubert Le Sueur for the casting of a Horse in Brasse bigger than a greate Horse by a foot; and the figure of His Maj. King Charles proportionable full six foot, which the afore saide Hubert Le Sueur is to perform with all the skill and workmanship as lieth in his powwer, and not onley shall be obliged to employ at the said Worcke such worckmen onder his direction as shall be skillfull able and caerfull for all the parts of the Worcke but also to cast the said Worck of the best Yealouw and red copper and caerfully provide for the strengthening and fearme ophoulding of the same, on the Pedestall were itt is to stand on.... The said Le Sueur is also to make a perfect Modell of the said Worcke, of the same

176. *Henri Quatre, King of France*. Franco-Italian, after a design by Gian da Bologna. Early seventeenth century. This is the only record we have in bronze of the appearance of the famous equestrian statue on the Pont-Neuf in Paris, which was destroyed during the Revolution. The actual work was done by Pietro Tacca and Pierre Franqueville, Gian's assistants and pupils.

bigness as the copper shall be, in the making wereof he shall take the advice of his Maj. Ridders of greate Horses, as well for the Shaep of the Horse and action as the graesfull shaep and action of his Maj. figure one the same. Which beeinge performed with the approbation of his Majt . . . the afore saide Le Sueur is to have for the intyre worck and full finisheing of the same in copper and setting in the place where it is to stand, the somme of six hundred pounds. . . .'

Intended at first for Covent Garden, Le Sueur was given eighteen months to finish the statue. It was cast in 1633 but had still not been erected at the King's death. During the Commonwealth it was sold for scrap-metal to a brass-founder named John Rivet of Holborn on condition that he should break it up, but Rivet buried the statue and showed a mass of broken bronze from which he proceeded to make souvenir knife-handles. From this he derived a great deal of profit, and after the Restoration he dug up the statue which was set in 1678 on a pedestal by Joshua Marshall, Master Mason to the Crown.

Grinling Gibbons (1648–1721) was the sculptor of statues of Charles II and James II, the former in Chelsea Hospital and the latter in Trafalgar Square. Both are in Roman armour, and have been given Roman hair-styles instead of the full-bottomed wig then fashionable. They were commissioned and paid for by Toby Rustate, Evelyn's 'very simple, ignorant, but honest and loyal creature'. Gibbon was paid £300 for *James II*, but it is doubtful whether he did more than design either of these statues. The actual work of modelling and casting was probably done by his assistants, Dievot of Brussels and Laurens of Mechlin.

Although the art of sculpture flourished in Holland during the seventeenth century, much of it was monumental and devoted to tombs of the rich and notable, and towards the end of the century craftsmen of all kinds followed William of Orange to England when he succeeded as William III. A good deal of work in an exaggerated Baroque style was done in the Low Countries during the seventeenth century.

In Germany the Thirty Years War, which began in 1618 and terminated with the Treaty of Westphalia in 1648, brought the art of sculpture to a temporary halt, particularly sculpture in bronze,

177. A river god representing the Nile. A reduction of a Graeco-Roman statue in the Vatican. French. Second half of the seventeenth century. Modern base. A pair of bronzes (this and the River Tiber) brought 991 *livres* (about £445) in the sale of Blondel de Gagny's effects in 1776.

since the metal was needed for the cannon-founder and armament-maker. Towards the end of the century, however, there was a revival, and from then onwards the bronze *Denkmal* was a favourite method of commemorating outstanding rulers and their subjects.

Notable is the equestrian statue of the Great Elector Frederick William of Brandenburg, who did much to repair his country's fortunes after the Thirty Years War. This, by Andreas Schluter (1664–1714), was inspired by Girardon's *Louis Quatorze*. It was formerly in the middle of the Long Bridge in Berlin, and has now been removed to the courtyard of the Charlottenburg, having survived the last war. At each of the four corners of the pedestal is a bronze slave, designed by Schluter and made by his pupils.

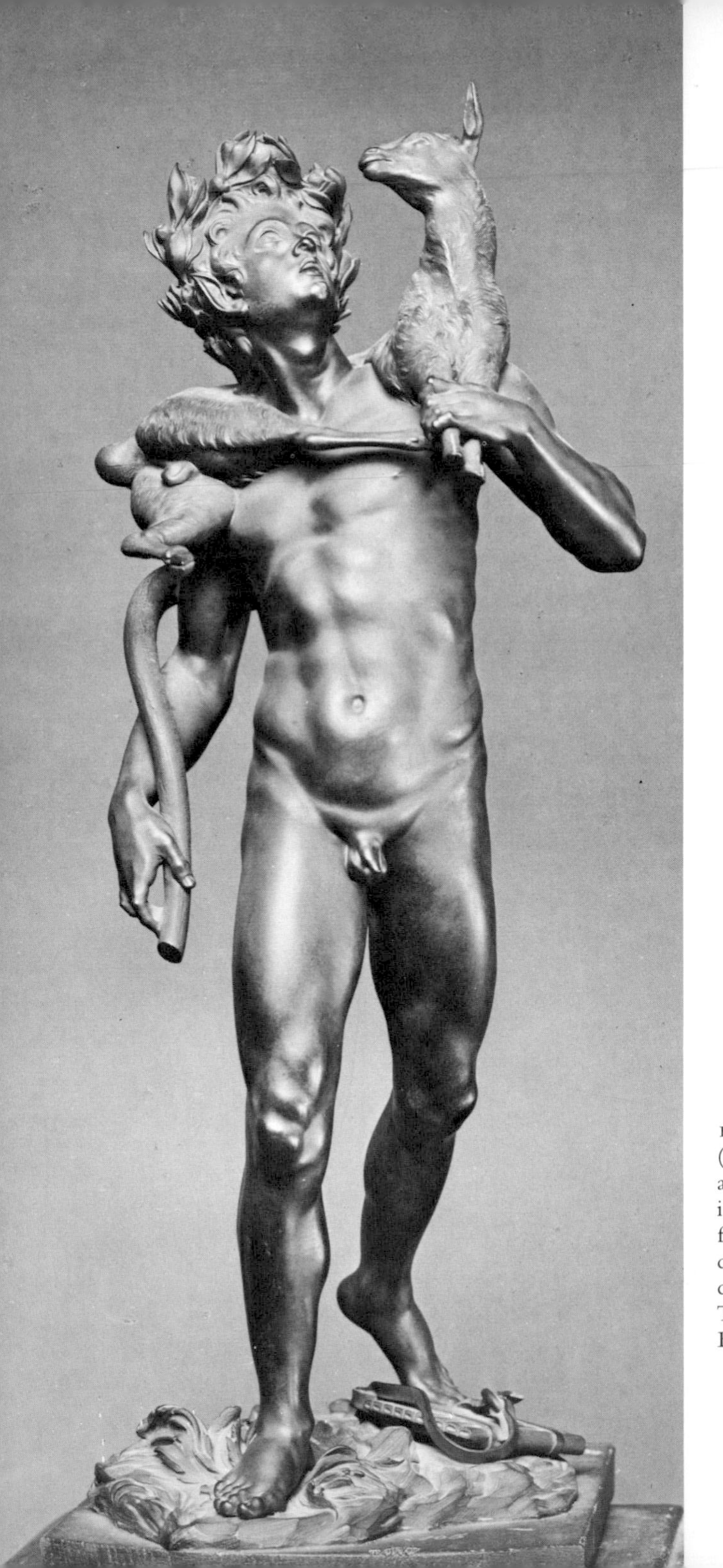

178. Massimiliano Soldani (1658–1740). *Faun*. Based on an antique model, this inspired the porcelain factories of the eighteenth century who produced both clothed and nude versions. The influence of Gian da Bologna is obvious.

CHAPTER SEVEN

The eighteenth century

There is nothing magical about the year 1700 to warrant its being used as a dividing line. The influence of Bernini still survived, and Massimiliano Soldani's *Faun*, done at the end of the seventeenth century, still harks back to Gian da Bologna in its adaptation of an antique original. A realistic division, however, could be made in 1715, with the death of Louis Quatorze and the beginning of the Régence, when the styles fashionable from *c.* 1690 onwards began to develop under the influence of the bronzeworkers in the direction of Rococo.

Ill. 178

The artistic capital of Europe had by this time been centred in Paris for many years past, and the broad outlines of eighteenth-century development had been laid down. The eighteenth century was to be the century of the bronzeworker, but not in quite the same way as the sixteenth, when statuary and bronze figures had been the most usual kind of decorative work in this metal. By far the greater amount of eighteenth-century work was in the form of more or less elaborate mounts for furniture and for *objets d'art* generally, and the practice of mounting objects of all kinds in gilded bronze instead of the precious metals was greatly extended.

Two names assume importance in the first half of the century, although neither of them were sculptors. Charles Cressent was a furniture-maker and bronzeworker; Juste-Aurele Meissonnier was a silversmith and a designer, as well as one of the more important influences contributing to the Rococo style.

Furniture of the eighteenth century often looks as though it had been designed by a metalworker, quite apart from the fact that much of it was heavily mounted with gilt-bronze. These furniture-mounts were not only decoration; they also had a very practical purpose. All of the finest furniture was at this time being decorated with veneers and marquetry – thin sheets of rare wood glued to a

179. Girardon. *Pluto carrying off Proserpine*. One of the groups designed by Le Brun for the gardens of Versailles. This model, twenty-one inches in height, and one of several known, was first produced in 1693. The large version was set up in 1699.

carcass of common wood. Bronze mounts, corner-pieces and fillets protected this delicate work from damage. Thus we find corner-pieces where two sheets of veneer meet, and fillets protecting other parts where the veneer was vulnerable. Bronze toes guard the bottoms of legs, and so forth.

Those *ébénistes* whose furniture is among the most outstanding usually made their own mounts, and Cressent was one of them. They did, however, become involved in frequent demarcation disputes with the Guild of *fondeurs-ciseleurs*, who contended that the making of mounts was their own sole prerogative. Most *ébénistes* perforce bought their mounts from members of the Guild, only those with the King's protection being exempt. Mounts, therefore,

180. Louis-Simon Boizot. *Pluto carrying off Proserpine*. A bronze version of a model made for the Sèvres porcelain factory, and exhibited in the Salon of 1786. It forms an interesting stylistic comparison with *Ill. 179*.

increasingly tended to fall into a series of stock patterns, usually based on one or other of the many design-books circulating at the time which were engraved and sold for the use of craftsmen of all kinds. These had started to proliferate in the second half of the seventeenth century, and designers become especially influential from this time onwards. They were an indispensable adjunct to manufactures of all kinds throughout the eighteenth century.

The vogue for mounting objects in gilt-bronze grew to a passion by mid-century, when everything was the subject of such mounting – porcelain, semi-precious stone, rare marbles, and even natural history curios like shells. Especially handsome are mounts characterized by the asymmetrical scrollwork which marks the Rococo style, and the account-books of Lazare Duvaux, art-dealer to the King and Mme de Pompadour, are full of references to mounted objects, or objects sent by customers to be mounted.

Clock-cases were handsome pieces of gilt-bronze, often elaborate examples of small sculpture with allegorical figures amid the scroll-work. This was a fashion perhaps started by André-Charles Boulle, but it continued unabated throughout the century, and persisted well into the following nineteenth century. Lighting appliances, from hand-candlesticks to elaborate candelabra and chandeliers, were hardly less sumptuous, the candelabra often in the form of figures upholding the candle-sockets. Contrasts of colour were attained by partial gilding and during the period of the Louis Seize style the bases, in the form of drum-pedestals, were often of bronze-mounted porcelain, or one or other of the semi-precious stones. But perhaps the most important examples of the bronzework of the period were the *chenets* or andirons which, in the days of Louis

181. Detail of the corner-piece of a *commode*. This kind of mount, known as an *espagnolette*, was associated with Charles Cressent, whose skill as a bronzeworker did much to establish the eighteenth-century French Court style in furniture decoration in its successful career.

182 (*right*). Wall-light. French. Mid eighteenth century. One of a set of four in the manner of Jacques Caffiéri. This, in a well-marked asymmetrical style characteristic of mid-century Rococo, is typical of the wall-lights of the period.

Quatorze, had often been of silver in the great houses. Bronze or gilt-bronze *chenets* were popular just before the beginning of the eighteenth century, but they were made in the greatest variety, and with an air of fantasy to be seen neither before nor after, at mid-century. We find many examples in Duvaux's account-books, like the pair depicting Love and a Vestal sold to Mme de Pompadour for Bellevue. The Prince de Condé had a pair in the Palais-Bourbon which depicted Chinese figures taking coffee that had cost him about £1,700 in today's money, and most were examples of small sculpture of extremely high quality by noted bronzeworkers of the

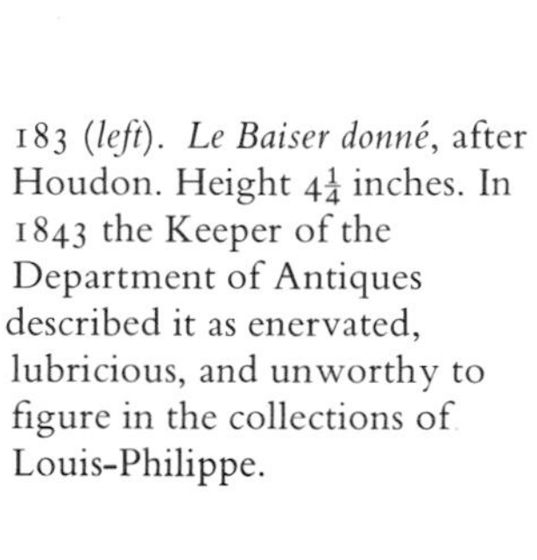

183 (*left*). *Le Baiser donné*, after Houdon. Height $4\frac{1}{4}$ inches. In 1843 the Keeper of the Department of Antiques described it as enervated, lubricious, and unworthy to figure in the collections of Louis-Philippe.

184 (*right*). *Le Baiser rendu*, after Houdon. A reduction of the well-known marble group, of which a number of versions exist. The theme of both these bronzes was suggested by a play by Taconet. The subject was employed by Falconet for two earlier groups in Sèvres porcelain.

day, or based on the work of the more fashionable sculptors and designed in the prevailing style of the period.

Gilding was by the mercuric process, referred to in contemporary records as *doré d'or moulu*, and this is the true meaning of the term *ormoulu*, already anglicized as 'ormolu' in the eighteenth century. This term has been very loosely applied since to alloys of all kinds. Gilding by this process often formed a disproportionate part of the cost of the complete work. For instance, in the case of an elaborately mounted bureau costing the equivalent of £2,700, about £575 was charged for chiselling the mounts after casting, and the same amount for gilding, leaving £1,650 to cover everything else, from the first model to the finished work. Bronzes were not always gilded however, and lacquering was sometimes employed as a finish. Occasionally some mounts were artificially patinated to resemble excavated bronze, a finish termed *verde antique*.

The best of the *fondeurs-ciseleurs* ranked very highly in the artistic hierarchy of their day. The names of Jacques and Philippe Caffiéri and Pierre Gouthière are familiar to all students of eighteenth-century French art. The *fondeurs* also worked for the sculptors of the time, casting their work in bronze, often from a marble or terracotta version, and making reductions.

Small sculpture was always fashionable – bronzes, marbles, and terracottas – for interior decoration, to stand on the top of a *sécrétaire* or on a *console* table. Jean-Baptiste Lemoyne (1704–78) belonged to a family of sculptors, and he was especially noted for his portrait busts, a fashionable revival of the old Roman custom exceedingly popular throughout the century. He was also the master of Jean-Jacques Caffiéri, another member of the well known family, who became chief modeller to the Sèvres porcelain factory, where mounting of the more important productions was commonly undertaken. Other famous pupils of Lemoyne were Falconet, Pajou, and Houdon.

Étienne-Maurice Falconet (1716–91) requires special notice. In his early work may be noticed the first tentative movements towards the new version of the Classical style to be seen soon after mid-century as a result of the discoveries at Pompeii and Herculaneum. He was influenced by the late seventeenth-century sculptor, Puget, even to the extent of selecting the latter's masterpiece, the *Milo of Croton*, as the subject for his own *morceau de reception* when he was

185. The famous equestrian statue of Peter the Great was first among the monuments of old St Petersburg, now Leningrad. It was produced by Falconet as a single casting. The total weight of bronze is sixteen tons, the metal varying between one inch and a quarter inch in thickness. The granite pedestal weighs fifteen hundred tons, and was hauled to the site on cannon-balls on an iron roadway by five hundred men.

PETRO PRIMO
CATHARINA SECUNDA
MDCCLXXXII

admitted to the Academy. A number of small bronzes exist from his hand, notably bronze versions of the marble *Baigneuse*, exhibited in the Salon of 1757, which was exceedingly popular and the subject of several porcelain versions.

In 1766 Falconet left for St Petersburg where he executed the great equestrian statue of Peter the Great for Catherine, with an unusual base of unhewn granite. This is one of the only two bronze equestrian statues by a French sculptor to survive the Revolution, the other being *Frederick V* by Jacques Saly at Copenhagen. Girardon's *Louis Quatorze* at Montpellier is a nineteenth-century replica.

Ill. 185

A notable example of eighteenth-century sculpture is to be found in the pair of horses done in marble *c.* 1740 for the entrance to the Marly riding-school, and brought to the Champs-Élysées in 1796. The sculptor was Guillaume I Coustou (1677–1746), a nephew of Coysevox. They are far better known from reductions in bronze, very variable in size, age, and quality, most being made during the nineteenth century for *bourgeois* chimney-pieces.

Ill. 186

Many of the sculptors of the time – Pigalle, Allegrain, Pajou, Clodion, Houdon, for example – worked in marble and terracotta, but bronze versions of many of their works are also to be found, moulded or reduced from the originals and cast by the *fondeurs*.

During the second half of the century, after the onset of the neo-Classical style, a few outstanding *fondeurs-ciseleurs* made bronze mounts distinguished for exceptional quality, of whom we may select Pierre Gouthière (1732–1813), who arrived in Paris in 1758 and later, as principal assistant, married the widow of his master, François Ceriset, a *maître-doreur*. This kind of marriage was an established practice in eighteenth-century France with the intention of continuing the workshop for the benefit of the widow, and there are many instances to be found among *ébénistes*, *fondeurs-ciseleurs*, and *faïenciers*.

Gouthière, one of the most successful bronzeworkers of his time, was much employed by Mme du Barry and Marie-Antoinette. Attested examples of his work, however, are very rare, although others are attributed to him on grounds of style, sometimes

186. One of the Marly Horses by Guillaume I Coustou. These reductions of the famous marble horses, done for the riding-school there, are contemporary, by or after Coustou. Numerous reductions have been made since, especially during the nineteenth century, many of poor quality.

Ill. 187 optimistically. A signed clock-case is in the Wallace Collection, and he is said to have made the elaborate bronze mounts used by the *ébéniste* Jean-Henri Riesener in his furniture for Marie-Antoinette, but this is uncertain.

Another well known bronzeworker of the period was Pierre Thomire (1751–1843), who worked as a *fondeur* for Pajou and Houdon and made furniture-mounts for Benemann. Later he organized the manufacture of bronzework of all kinds on almost factory lines as Thomire-Dutherme et Cie.

The manufacture of such things as furniture-mounts and ornamental clock-cases was organized on similar lines in England by Boulton & Fothergill of Soho, Birmingham, who competed with the French *fondeurs* in the Russian market. Wedgwood visited Boulton's factory in 1776, and left a description of it in a letter to his partner, Bentley: 'I had no conception of the quantity of D'Or Moulu they have sold, chiefly abroad, you remember a poor Venus weeping over the Tomb of Adonis – a Time Piece. How many would you imagine they have sold of this single group? 200 at 25 guineas each [about £250 today], including the watch. They now sell as much of this manufacture as they can get up. Mr Boulton told me that they now had very great influence at the Russian Court . . . and they hoped to supplant the French in the Gilt business.'

English manufacturers also exported mounts to France, and catalogues preserved in Victoria and Albert Museum belonging to the early years of the nineteenth century list lustres, candelabra, lamps, inkstands, flower-vases, and paperweights of bronze or 'Ormolu'. A catalogue of 1785 mentions 'French handles' for furniture, and 'Escutcheons to match the French handles', and some of the French furniture in the Museum is fitted with handles closely resembling those shown in the catalogue. Probably they were exported in an unfinished state and chiselled in France. Records of 1777 show that thirty-odd brass-founders of Birmingham were using between them about a thousand tons of brass annually, no doubt made with zinc from Bristol, where William Champion was producing about two hundred tons a year in 1740. Brass-founders were established in Birmingham from 1689 onwards.

187. *The Avignon Clock* symbolizing the rivers Rhône and Durance, designed by Boizot and executed by Gouthière. The former received 1500 *livres* for the model, and the latter 9200 *livres* for the casting, chiselling, and gilding 'de la manière la plus riche'.

In the early years of the eighteenth century decorative sculpture became extremely fashionable in London, and workshops sprang up to supply the demand. Among them was that of John van Ost (or Nost) who made a gilt-bronze statue of George I for Grosvenor Square in 1726 which disappeared before 1850. Sir Henry Cheere (b. 1703), and his brother John, maintained a foundry at Hyde Park Corner, next to the studio of Peter Scheemakers (1691–1770), where they cast in lead and bronze as well as carving in marble. Whether by arrangement, or by simple piracy, the Cheeres cast at least two of Rysbrack's marble carvings in bronze.

Rysbrack himself was almost solely a marble-carver, and a modeller in terracotta. He completed one important work in bronze – the equestrian statue of William III at Bristol which owes something to *Marcus Aurelius*, and it is also hardly surprising that a plaster model of Girardon's *Louis Quatorze* appeared in Rysbrack's sale of 1767. John Bacon, RA revived the earlier Greek method of making bronzes in sections, fusing them together afterwards, but contemporary criticism of one of the works made in this way suggests that the method in his hands was hardly a satisfactory one.

After the beginning of the fashion for neo-Classicism, marked by the onset of the Adam style, white marble was increasingly favoured for sculpture, and this was the product of two misapprehensions, the first that the Greeks and Romans employed white marble for statuary when, in fact, they coloured it, and the second, that they commonly employed marble for statuary when, in fact, they gave equal importance to bronze, and probably valued it more highly.

In Germany modelling for porcelain provided a lucrative occupation for many sculptors, and since most of the factories were owned by the rulers of the German States, Court Sculptors were frequently thus employed. Bronzes were much valued, however, and the Bronze Room at the royal palace of Augustus in Dresden housed more than a hundred small bronzes belonging to the period between the sixteenth and the eighteenth century, many of which had formed part of the collection of Augustus the Strong. A gilded bronze statue of Augustus in Dresden Neustadt was the work of a cannon-founder, Captain Ludwig Wiedmann of Augsburg, and the same

188. The persisting influence of Bernini is to be observed in this Virgin and Child of gilded bronze. with a rose marble background. From Bologna, *c.* 1750. The Arms are those of Benedict XLV, elected 1741, died 1748.

officer, now promoted to Colonel, came to England in 1748 to demonstrate an improved method of casting bronze cannon at the New Foundry in Chelsea before the Duke of Cumberland. His cannon failed under test, and one of them burst. Three are still preserved at Woolwich Arsenal.

In Italy Antonio Canova (1757–1822) became the leader of a group of neo-Classical sculptors which included Flaxman and Thorwaldsen, all of whom lived and worked in Rome. Canova, an exceptionally generous man, assisted many of the sculptors who flocked to Rome in the second half of the eighteenth century following the discoveries at Herculaneum and Pompeii, and the publication of Winckelmann's books. Canova, like most other neo-Classical sculptors, made little use of bronze, but a statue in this metal of Napoleon I as a Roman Emperor is in the courtyard of the Palazzo di Brera in Milan.

In general, Italian sculpture during the eighteenth century became notable for poverty of design and inspiration, and very little work in bronze was undertaken. The passion for public monuments became entirely out of hand in nineteenth-century Italy, with those of Garibaldi and Victor Emmanuel proliferating on every side. The country had by then become a vast museum, attracting sculptors from all over the world to study the art of the past.

CHAPTER EIGHT

The nineteenth century and after

The nineteenth century saw the introduction of such methods as electrotyping which, by enabling bronzes to be reproduced cheaply and accurately, ensured that they decorated every *bourgeois* interior in profusion – reductions of statuary of all kinds, and copies of eighteenth-century work, especially chimney-piece ornaments and clock-cases. From Italy came numerous copies of antique sculpture of variable quality, some of which, like the *Dancing Faun*, may be found decorating modern suburban gardens, while foundries at Naples specialized in copies of ancient statuary excavated at Pompeii and Herculaneum, which were made in all sizes. It was not bronze that was scarce in the nineteenth century but contemporary work of noteworthy quality.

The change was as much social as artistic. The new *bourgeoisie* who had money to spend possessed neither the traditions of the aristocracy nor the *panache* of such mercantile families as the Fuggers and the Medicis in their early days. The modern State, protected at every point by a bureaucracy armoured with paper, was replacing older forms of government. Statuary was no longer commissioned by a single man of taste, but by committees of mediocrities who glibly pronounced on the sculptor's designs with an ignorance matched only by audacity. After Waterloo the disciplines of neo-Classicism were progressively abandoned, and the Empire style of Napoleon I, based on that of Imperial Rome, only lingered in the work of a few sculptors of the period, such as François Rude (1784–1855), born at Dijon, the son of a coppersmith. His *Mercury tying his sandals* is in the Louvre.

Antoine-Louis Barye (1796–1875) is more interesting as representing a new departure in bronze sculpture. Barye was apprenticed to a goldsmith, and before he was out of his time he had begun to model small figures of animals. He extended his studies to zoological gardens and horse-fairs, dissecting such specimens as came his way to improve his anatomical knowledge. Unrecognized in academic circles, he established his own bronze-foundry, casting many of his models himself. His foundry also made decorative objects – candelabra and clocks – often decorated with animals, as well as mounts of all kinds. As a sculptor of animals he has only rarely been excelled and his large bronzes of animal combats are well conceived and executed with spirit. His human figures are less successful. Barye was skilled in the colouring and patination of bronzes, and his work founded a French school of animal sculpture in bronze – the *Animaliers* – which included Emmanuel Frémiet, August-Nicolas Cain, Georges Gardet, and Pierre-Jules Méne. Frémiet also executed commissions for large monumental statuary.

Ill. 189

Bronzes cast by Barye, or by his assistant Gonon and his sons, are extremely fine in quality, but numerous copies were made by Émile Martin between 1848 and 1857 by sand-casting, and later versions by Barye himself are noticeably poorer in quality and were probably cast in the same way. Sand-casting was a method much employed for cheap *bronzes d'ameublement* in the middle of the nineteenth century but the quality is very much poorer than lost wax casts.

The work of Barye later influenced that of Rodin, and the bronze group, the *Death of Ugolini and his Sons* by Jean-Baptiste Carpeaux (1827–75), now in the Louvre, probably inspired Rodin's choice of the same subject for his bronze door, the *Porte d'Enfer*. Carpeaux's version depicts Ugolino and his sons dying from hunger, and portrays the Count gnawing his fingers. Rodin shows him, blind and naked, crawling on hands and knees over the bodies of his sons.

Ill. 191

Jules Dalou (1838–1902) studied with Carpeaux, and became a political refugee in London in 1871, where he had a professorship at the old South Kensington Museum. Derivations from his hand of the figures in the popular paintings by Millet started a new fashion for bronzes of peasants which were produced in large numbers. Dalou was also addicted to pompous allegory.

By now the industry was almost entirely on a commercial footing, reproducing a variety of subjects in large quantities, all of them

189. Antoine-Louis Barye (1796–1875). *Jaguar devouring an alligator.* Barye, who was the first of the *Animaliers,* excelled as a sculptor of animals, and he was especially skilled in the colouring and patination of bronze.

calculated to appeal to popular taste. Sculptors did little more than provide the model, and the work of finishing was only done by them on important works. Bronze-founders in Paris were skilled in colouring as well as casting. An alloy in common use was composed of eighty per cent of copper, seventeen per cent of zinc, and three per cent of tin and lead, which is indistinguishable from brass. By mid-century about six thousand men were continuously employed in Paris alone on this kind of work, and their products were exported freely. Many of them appeared in the Great Exhibition of 1851.

Despite the unfavourable conditions prevailing a few artists of stature arose after mid-century as a reaction against the tasteless clutter of official art. Auguste Rodin (1840–1917) was born the son of a minor civil servant. He began to study at the Petit École de Dessin at an early age, and attended a class directed by Barye. Lacking both money and influence he was compelled to work in a plasterer's workshop trimming mould-marks and cleaning up casts. Rodin's first work, produced in a studio which he set up in an old

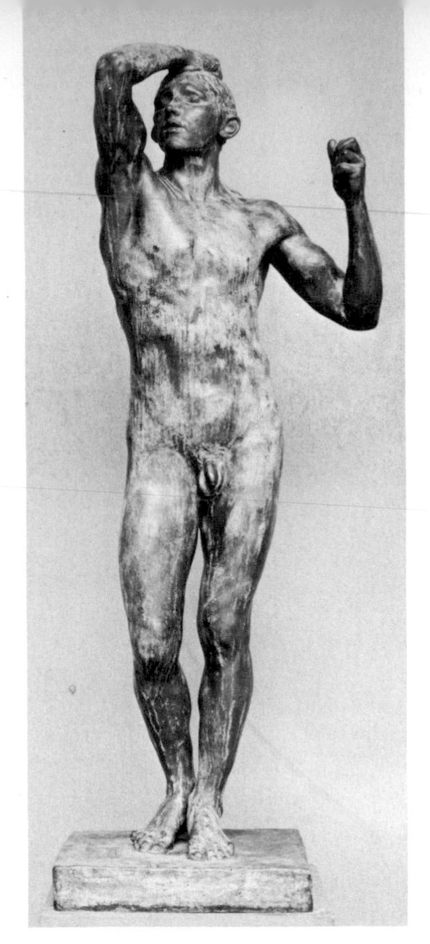

190. Auguste Rodin. *The Age of Bronze*. This is Rodin's first major work, and one which provoked a good deal of criticism when it was first exhibited in the Cercle Artistique in 1877. It is one of a number of copies.

191 *La Porte d'Enfer*, by Rodin. Conceived as a kind of antithesis to Ghiberti's *Gates of Paradise*, it was commissioned for the Musée des Arts Décoratifs in 1880, and unfinished when Rodin died in 1917. Several well known sculptures by Rodin started as part of its design.

stable, was the mask of *The Man with the Broken Nose*, sufficient evidence of the direction of his thoughts, and this was accepted in the Salon of 1878 after having been rejected in 1864. Rodin supported himself by taking employment with Carrier-Belleuse, a commercial sculptor who worked for the porcelain factories, and Rodin himself worked for Sèvres.

After 1870 Rodin passed a period of study in Italy devoting himself to Renaissance sculpture, and came to be convinced that the only true inspiration lay in the study of the living model rather than the antique. Influenced by both Michelangelo and Donatello he modelled a male nude, *The Age of Bronze*, which had a mixed

Ill. 190

reception from critics at the exhibition of the Cercle Artistique in 1877. It was this work which became the subject of the charge that it was a cast from life – a common enough procedure in the history of sculpture, the most frequent example of which is the death-mask. In this context, however, the charge was tantamount to one of fraud and incompetence, and to prove his ability he executed a *St John the Baptist* which is much larger than life.

It is evident that Rodin had little sympathy with academic sculpture, and at the time life in France was singularly difficult for a sculptor who lacked academic support. A good friend, M. Edmond Turquet, who was Under-Secretary of State for the Fine Arts, commissioned a bronze door, eighteen feet in height, intended for the Musée des Arts Decoratifs which remained uncompleted at Rodin's death thirty-seven years later. The subject he selected was the Gate of Hell – *La Porte d'Enfer* – based on Dante's *Inferno* and intended to be the antithesis of Ghiberti's Gate of Paradise. He did not, however, adhere to the same scheme of a series of panels, modelling two main panels, largely in high relief. To these doors we can trace the inspiration of a number of later works in bronze and marble. The old woman naked, known as *La Belle Heaulmière*, is from this source, as well as such works as *La Jeune Mère* of 1885, *L'Hombre* of 1880, and *Le Baiser*, the *bête noir* of English provincial Aldermen which is actually an illustration of an episode from Dante, the figures representing Paolo Malatesta and Francesca da Rimini.

Ill. 191

Ill. 192

In his designs for these doors Rodin seems to have been influenced not only by Dante but by the feverish imagination of Baudelaire. It is also possible to see the influence of Carpeaux, and from Barye he may have taken his habit of defining the parts of the figure to which he wished to lend particular significance. It is to Rodin that we owe a development which has been well called 'the significance of the fragment'. The torso by itself appears as an independent theme

192. Rodin. *Le Baiser*. Bronze version. This group, which started as part of the design for *La Porte d'Enfer*, illustrates the story of Paolo Malatesta and Francesca da Rimini from Dante's *Inferno*.

for the first time in the work of Rodin, and this he developed in the direction of such subjects as *La Main de Dieu* of 1898. He also excelled in the representation of movement which, like Gian da Bologna before him, he employed to excite curiosity from all angles of view, to which he added the technique of breaking up the surface into light-reflecting facets in a manner more recently familiar in some of the bronzes of Epstein. This may have been suggested in the first place by some of the rare bronzes of Daumier. *Ill. 194*

Towards the end of his life Rodin turned increasingly to marble, and replicas of his more outstanding bronzes are fairly numerous. A few of his marbles also exist in a bronze version, for instance the one illustrated here.

193 (*left*). Edgar Degas. *Dancer.* Some of these dancers, closely related in pose, can reasonably be regarded as part of the evolution of the same study. They can tentatively be dated by relating them to paintings of similar subjects.

194 (*right*). Honoré Daumier. *Ratapoil.* Cast by Valsuani. Daumier turned to modelling in clay as an aid to his work as a political caricaturist. This is a cast of one such model, made about 1850.

Ill. 193

The bronzes of Degas were preserved almost by accident. Few people in his lifetime even knew that he modelled, hardly anything was cast in plaster, and nothing in bronze. After his death in 1917 about one hundred and fifty models in wax or clay were found in his studio, but only about seventy were in a fit state to cast. The others had dried out, were cracked, or were too badly damaged to reclaim. The best were placed in the hands of the bronze-founder Hébrard who cast them between 1919 and 1921, wherever possible in the state in which they were found. A few were repaired by the sculptor Bartholomé. Seventy-three were cast altogether in editions of twenty-two. The twenty for sale were marked with the letters A to T, one unlettered copy was retained by the founder, and one went to the artist's heirs, the latter being marked *HER*. Each model was numbered from 1 to 72; the seventy-third, cast later, was unnumbered. Each has the incised signature of Degas and the stamp of the founder, A.-A. Hébrard.

The bronzes of Degas include horses, youthful ballet-dancers, portrait heads and busts, and bathers. Little is known of the period at which they were executed, but some have been tentatively dated by relating them to paintings of similar subjects. Many were rapid sketches to provide studies for painting, but others were deliberate works of sculpture. All of them have exceptional qualities of life and movement, and Renoir referred to Degas 'as the greatest living sculptor', ranking him above Rodin.

Ill. 195 Aristide Maillol (1861–1944) spans the nineteenth and twentieth centuries. His sculpture, much of it in bronze, reverts to the ideals of fifth-century Greece instead of the changing, fluid forms of Rodin or the highly-finished derivations from Greek and Roman work

195. The work of Aristide Maillol (1861–1944), here represented by a *Torso* of 1905–6 cast by Alexis Rudier, is a reversion to the ideals of fifth-century Greece.

which were the product of neo-Classicism. Most of Maillol's work is devoted to the female nude, and Jean Renoir relates that when Maillol was asked to do a monument to Zola he suggested a statue of his wife, Clotilde, in the nude, adding that her body was so much more beautiful than Zola's.

In his later years Renoir himself turned to sculpture, but his hands had been so crippled by arthritis that he was compelled to work through the medium of an Italian assistant, Guino, and then with the help of Marcel-Antoine Gimond, who made a portrait bust on the day of Renoir's death.

Ill. 196

The nineteenth century in England had little of importance to show. Matthew Coates Wyatt (1777–1862) first designed a *quadriga* as a suitable vehicle for a statue of George III, but insufficient money was forthcoming and it ended as the equestrian statue in Cockspur Street, near the National Gallery, which departed from custom by depicting the King in modern dress. Sir Edwin Henry Landseer

196. Pierre-Auguste Renoir. *La Laveuse*. c. 1917–18. Renoir turned to sculpture in 1913 at the suggestion of Vollard, making small models with the intention of having them cast in a larger size. His modelling was not without an effect on his later painting.

(1802–73), best known as a painter of sentimentally contrived animal subjects, modelled the amiable and clumsy lions on the four corners of the base of Nelson's Column, which were cast in 1868 by the Baron Marochetti, who exhibited a spirited equestrian plaster model of that leader of crusading *banditti*, Richard Cœur de Lion, in the Great Exhibition of 1851 which was later cast in bronze. *Boadicea* at Westminster Bridge by Thomas Thorneycroft (1815–85) was cast in 1897. Alfred Gilbert (1854–1934), who studied in Paris and Rome, worked first in a revived Renaissance style popular after 1870, turning afterwards to *Art Nouveau*. His most widely known work, the Piccadilly *Eros*, is aluminium, not bronze, and was perhaps the first public statue to be cast in this metal. His masterpiece, however, is probably the Tomb of the Duke of Clarence at Windsor, an amazing creation of writhing and undulating forms.

George Frederick Watts (1817–1904) was also a sculptor whose work is, perhaps, more notable than that of many of his con-

197. Gilt-bronze lamp in the Art Nouveau style, apparently inspired by a bronze by Paul Roche, representing the dancer, Loïs Fuller, in characteristic pose. Paris. *c.* 1900.

198. George Frederick Watts. *Clytie*. *c*. 1868–80. Watts studied in the studio of the sculptor, William Behnes, and his few works of sculpture are perhaps more acceptable than his almost forgotten paintings.

temporaries. His largest work is the heroic equestrian statue symbolizing Physical Energy in Kensington Gardens which also forms the central part of the Cecil Rhodes Memorial at Cape Town. His portrait bust called *Clytie* was also cast in bronze. *Ill. 198*

England may, perhaps, fairly lay claim to Sir Jacob Epstein (1880–1959), although he was born in Brooklyn and did not come to

199. Sir Jacob Epstein. *Kitty*. Epstein freely acknowledged his debt to Rodin, but this does not lessen his stature as the greatest of twentieth-century portrait sculptors in bronze.

England until 1905. Until his later years he had little reason for gratitude to his adopted country. His work was the subject of ignorant jeers, and of libellous misrepresentation in the popular Press. His best work is undoubtedly the portraits in bronze which owe something to the influence of Rodin – a debt which Epstein freely acknowledged. He also sought inspiration in ancient and primitive sculpture, of which he had a notable collection. He must undoubtedly be numbered among the leading sculptors of modern times.

Ill. 199

The passion for the *Denkmal* was strong in Germany, of which the thirteen-foot-high surviving monument to Bismarck near the Brandenburger Tor in Berlin is an example. This, unveiled in 1903, was the work of Professor Robert Diez. The art of metal-casting had been brought to a very high degree of excellence in Berlin before the middle of the nineteenth century, when the Royal Prussian Foundry was celebrated for casting objects of all kinds, some of great intricacy. The progress made in the technical aspects was remarkable. Ferdinand von Müller of the Royal Bronze Foundry at Munich, where the bronze doors of the Capitol at Washington were made, was a skilled bronze-founder, about whose colossal lion (one of four), nine feet high and fifteen feet long, a contemporary wrote, 'As a specimen of metal-casting this lion is no less remarkable than as a work of art, no file, chisel, or other tool having touched his hide since he was born in a hot mould' – an extraordinary feat.

Colossal statuary is represented by the *Bavaria* of Ludwig Schwanthaler in Munich, which is fifty feet high and ninety-eight feet with the pedestal, with a weight estimated at 125 tons. This, also, was cast by von Müller.

Casting in zinc alone became a Berlin speciality. The cost was about one-sixth of that of a bronze cast, principally owing to the much lower melting-point of the metal. Zinc casts were inferior to those of bronze, both in sharpness of detail and in colour, but this disadvantage was overcome by bronzing – the speciality of a certain Herr Geiss. Electrotyping was also done in Berlin on a large scale. Troughs twelve feet long to contain moulds and electrolyte, and proportionately wide, were in use at the principal factories, and in this way the process was employed to reproduce works of major size. By 1850 three firms in particular are recorded as doing work of this kind – Winkelmann, Sussmann, and Möhring – who were well in advance of those working elsewhere.

Twentieth-century sculpture has shared the universal passion of the age for novelty, and it has been notable for the experimental use of new materials. There has, on the whole, been a movement away from casting and towards such constructive techniques as welding, the consequence perhaps of an increasing use of iron, which Picasso was employing tentatively before the last war. This necessarily results in a different kind of object, which is usually abstract or semi-abstract. The making of large works in sections subsequently joined in one way or another is an ancient technique, but these were a translation into a much greater size of the sculptor's model or maquette, and the work of giving it its final form was often as much the task of the craftsman as of the sculptor himself.

The use of iron has brought with it an entirely new conception of the nature and purpose of sculpture, and much of it has been well described as three-dimensional drawing. The metal, however, has many disadvantages, not the least that it must be protected from rust.

The development, however, is probably a transitory one, and it is likely that the sculptor will return to bronze as the most satisfactory metal for his purpose, both for its appearance and for the

200. A very rare bronze by Georges Braque. *Cheval*. 1939. One of six casts. In form it is reminiscent of *Ill. 24*.

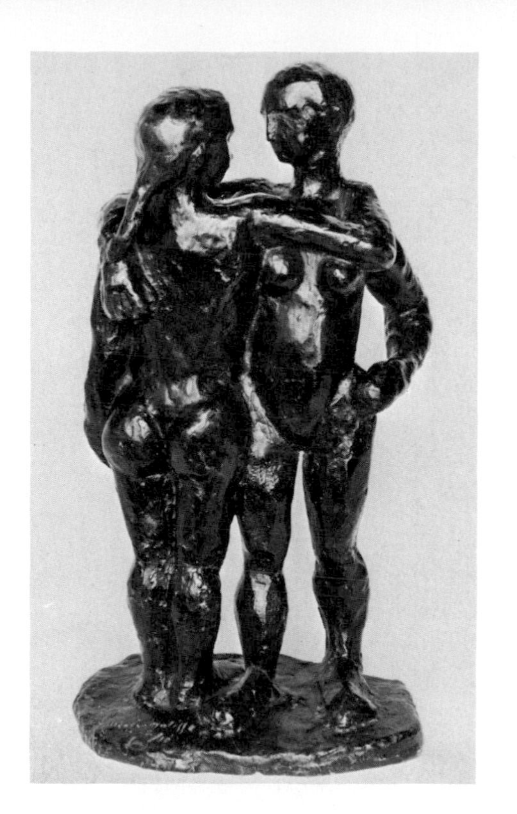

201. Henri Matisse. *Deux Négresses*. 1908. The seventh of ten copies, with the stamp of the caster, Valsuani. This, the only group of two figures modelled by Matisse, has been influenced by West African sculpture.

advantages conferred in the actual making of an object. None of the modern materials are as adaptable to the requirements of casting.

There is only space to mention a few of the sculptors of the present century who have employed bronze as a medium. The work of Henri Matisse was largely devoted to the female nude, and most of his bronzes seem to have been made between 1905 and 1911 and again between 1925 and 1930. About seventy exist, of which an example is illustrated here. Bronzes from the hand of Georges Braque are rare, but one obviously influenced by the Greek Archaic period is shown. Generally, six copies of each work were cast, although in at least one instance seven were made. Most were cast in the 1950s from plaster models made before 1939.

Ill. 201

Ill. 200

The limited number of bronzes from Paul Gauguin are a product of the fashion for the sculpture of primitive peoples which has influenced so many sculptors of the twentieth century, to which the continuing demand for the West African bronzes of Benin that first reached Europe at the turn of the century testifies. Gauguin's rare bronzes are casts of woodcarvings – an origin obvious from their form and treatment.

Ill. 202 A good deal of Picasso's early sculpture is in bronze, cast from plaster originals; in his later work he turned to less traditional materials. Although Picasso is the principal sculptor associated with

202. Pablo Picasso. *Buste d'une femme* (a portrait of Fernande Olivier). Signed. This bust was executed in 1905 and is the fifth of ten casts made by Valsuani.

203 (*left*). Ossip Zadkine (1890–1968). *Standing Woman.* 1920. Zadkine, a Russian, studied in England and moved to Paris in 1909, where he became one of the earliest of the Cubist sculptors.

204 (*right*). Jacques Lipchitz (b. 1891). *Guitar Player.* 1918. Lipchitz arrived in Paris about the same time as Zadkine, and was also influenced by Cubism. He went to America in 1941.

the Cubist movement, both Jacques Lipchitz and Ossip Zadkine have done notable work of this kind. *Ills. 203, 204*

The widespread vogue for abstraction in painting is inimical to the traditional sculptural treatment of the living body, and from the early years of the present century the tendency for sculptors to employ abstractions only distantly recalling natural forms has continually increased. This is to be observed in the work of Henry

Moore, both in his large sculpture intended for outdoor settings, and in his small bronzes produced in limited editions. The influence of the past, however, is not entirely lacking in the work of Henry Moore and others. Moore's *Warrior with Shield* of 1954 was perhaps unconsciously inspired by the mutilated appearance of some excavated early statuary.

Ill. 206

The equestrian statue in its contemporary form is to be found in the small bronze sculpture of Marino Marini, although one example of 1949, for instance, seems to have been much more influenced by Chinese pottery tomb-figures of the fifth century AD than by Western equestrian subjects. The elongated figures of Alberto Giacometti recall the somewhat similar treatment of certain early Etruscan votive bronzes, and the encrusted surfaces also bear a colourable resemblance to excavated bronze.

Ill. 205

205. Marino Marini (b. 1901). *Horse and Rider.* 1947. Marini's most important works are variations on this theme. His sculptures of human figures are less successful.

206. Henry Moore (b. 1898). *Warrior with Shield.* 1953–54. Moore now dominates the modern movement in sculpture. His major works in bronze are subsequent to 1945.

Ill. 209 The sculpture of Jean Arp on the other hand, done relatively late in his career, is almost completely abstract; he was influenced by the earlier sculpture of Brancusi who was the first to turn to pure form with little or no relationship to the forms of nature.

Among the more remarkable manifestations of twentieth-century neurosis are the bronzes of Germaine Richier which, based on natural forms, are both alien and sinister, like something from a remote part of the universe. Barely human, her figures are clumsily posed on stick-like limbs resembling those of insects, with faces disintegrating in necrotic decay. *Ill. 208*

From Germany have come notable bronzes by Ernst Barlach who died in 1938. Barlach was an Expressionist whose woodcarvings and bronzes reflect a fifteenth-century tradition. He owed something

207. Wilhelm Lehmbruck (1881–1919). *Young Man Seated*. 1918. Lehmbruck's work is noted principally for the graceful pose of his elongated figures.

208. Germaine Richier (1904–1959). *The Wasp*. 1953. Her work is often a mixture of human, animal, and vegetable forms.

also to the Russian peasant figure, a product of an early visit to the USSR. A few bronzes from his hand still exist, but much of his work was destroyed by the Nazis. Wilhelm Lehmbruck, who died in 1919, is especially noted for nudes in bronze, and Karl Hartung was influenced by Maillol in his early work, but later turned to abstract sculpture. *Ill. 207*

Generally, contemporary sculpture owes little to the past. Whether present experiments are likely to survive it is too early to judge. Much modern work is pessimistic in its approach, and some, like the work of Richier, is nightmarish. It is hard to resist the conclusion that the art of sculpture is being called upon to express ideas and notions which are foreign to its nature, and which would be better expressed by other means. For this reason, if for no others, an eventual return to the mainstream of tradition which served humanity well for more than four thousand years ought not to be dismissed as entirely unlikely.

209.
Jean Arp (1886–1966).
Ptolemy I. 1953.

Bibliography

List of Illustrations

Index

Bibliography

Agricola. *De re metallica.* English translation 1912

Alexander, W. & Street, A. *Metals in the Service of Man.* Harmondsworth 1956

Barnard, Noël. *Bronze casting and bronze alloys in ancient China.* Melbourne 1961

Barth, Hans-Martin. *Die Sebalduskirche in Nürnberg.* Königstein-im-Taunus. (N.D. recent)

Bechstein, Hanns. *Honoré Daumier: Der Parlement der Juli-Monarchie.* Berlin 1959

Bénézit, E. *Dictionnaire critique et documentaire des peintres, sculpteurs . . . de France.* Paris 1911–23

Bode, Wilhelm von. *Florentine sculptors of the Renaissance.* London 1908
Italian Bronze Statuettes of the Renaissance. London 1907–12

Boffrand, Germain. *Description de ce qui a été pratiqué pour fondre en bronze, d'un seul jet, la figure équestre de Louis XIV, elevée par la ville de Paris dans la place Louis-le-Grand.* Paris 1745

Bonnin, A. *Tutenag and Paktong.* Oxford 1925

British Museum. *Guide to Medieval Antiquities.* London 1924

British Museum. *Guide to the Antiquities of the Bronze Age.* London 1904

British Museum. *A general guide to the Egyptian collections.* London 1930

Burlington Fine Arts Club. *Catalogue of an Exhibition of Counterfeits, Imitations, and Copies.* London 1924

Casson, Stanley. *The Technique of Early Greek Sculpture.* Oxford 1933

Cellini, Benvenuto. *Trattati dell'orificeria e della scultura.* Florence 1857. English translation by C. R. Ashbee, 1898
Memoirs. (Various English editions)

Crutwell, M. *Antonio Pollaiuolo.* London 1907
Verrocchio. London 1904

Davies, O. *Roman mines in Europe.* Oxford 1935

Diderot, D. & D'Alembert, J. de R. *Encyclopédie des Sciences, des arts, et des métiers.* 17 vols and 11 vols of plates, and 5 supplementary volumes. Paris 1751–77

Diodorus Siculus. *History.* (Booth's translation.) London 1824

Düsseldorf Kunstmuseum. Exhibition Catalogue. *Deutsche Bronzen des Mittelalters und der Renaissance.* 1960

Encyclopédie photographique de l'art. (Louvre Museum) – Egypt, Mesopotamia, Greece, and Italy. 3 vols. Paris 1935

Epstein, Sir Jacob. *Let there be sculpture.* London 1942

Forbes, R. J. *Metallurgy in Antiquity.* Leiden 1950

Fortnum, C. Drury. *Bronzes.* London 1877

Gardner, E. A. *Handbook of Greek Sculpture.* 2 vols. London 1907

Garner, Sir Harry. *Chinese and Japanese cloisonné enamels.* London 1962

Germanisches Museum. *Deutsche Kunst und Kultur.* Nürnberg 1960

Giacommetti, Georges. *Le statuaire Jean-Antoine Houdon et son époque (1741–1828).* Paris 1918

Girschmann, R. *Iran.* Harmondsworth 1954

Godard, A. *L'Art de l'Iran.* Paris 1962

Gowland, Professor W. *Metals and Metallurgy in Old Japan.* Transactions of the Japan Society, vol. XIII. 1915

Guiffrey, J. J. *Les Caffiéri, sculpteurs et fondeurs-ciseleurs.* Paris 1877

Higgins, R. *Minoan and Mycenaean Art.* London 1967

Hill, A. A. *A corpus of Italian medals of the Renaissance before Cellini.* 2 vols. Oxford 1930

Hodges, E. *Artifacts. An introduction to early materials and technology.* London 1964

Jenyns, Soame & Watson, William. *Chinese Art.* Vol. II. London 1963

Josephus, Flavius. *Antiquities of the Jews.* Translation by Whiston. (Various editions)

Kahnweiler, D. H. *The sculpture of Picasso.* London 1949

Karlgren, Bernhard. *New studies in Chinese bronzes.* Stockholm 1937

Museum of Far Eastern Antiquities, Stockholm. Bulletin. No. 8. 1936

Lamb, Winifred. *Greek and Roman Bronzes.* London 1928

Lane-Poole, Stanley. *The Art of the Saracens.* London 1886

Lion-Goldschmidt, D. & Gobard, M. *Chinese Art.* Vol. I. London 1961

S. Magdalenen, Hildesheim. (Author unknown.) Stuttgart 1962

Maspero, G. *Guide to the Cairo Museum.* (French Institute.) Cairo 1910

Needham, Joseph. *Science and Civilization in China.* Cambridge. (Volumes in course of publication)

Oman, Charles. *The Gloucester Candlestick.* London 1958

Petrie, W. M. Flinders. *The Arts and Crafts of Egypt.* London (reprinted 1923)

Planiscig, Leo. *Piccoli bronzi italiani del Rinascimento.* Milan 1930

Kunsthistorisches Museum in Wien: Die Bronzeplastiken. Vienna 1924

Andrea del Verrocchio. Vienna 1941

Plenderleith, Dr H. J. *Technical notes on Chinese bronzes.* Transactions of the Oriental Ceramic Society. 1938–39

Pliny the Elder (Gaius Plinius Secundus). *Natural History*. (Various translations)

Pope-Henessy, J. *Italian Renaissance Sculpture*. London 1958
Italian High Renaissance and Baroque Sculpture. London 1963

Read, Herbert. *Concise History of Modern Sculpture*. London 1964

Réau, Louis. *Etienne-Maurice Falconet*. Paris 1923

Redcliffe, A. *European Bronze Statuettes*. London 1966

Reeves, Ruth. *Cire Perdue casting in India*. New Delhi 1962

Rewald, John. *Degas. Sculpture*. London 1957

Rich, J. C. *Materials and methods of sculpture*. Oxford 1947

Salmony, A. *Sino-Siberian Art*. Paris 1923

Sauerländer, W. *Die Skulptur des Mittelalters*. Berlin 1963

Tavernor-Parry, J. *Dinanderie*. London 1910

Theophilus. *De diversis artibus*. Translated by C. R. Dodwell. London 1961

Thompson, R. C. *A dictionary of Assyrian chemistry and geology*. Oxford 1936

Vasari, Giorgio. *Lives of the Painters, Sculptors, and Architects*. (Various editions)

Verlet, Pierre. *French Royal Furniture*. London 1963
French Furniture and Interior Decoration of the 18th century. London 1967

Victoria and Albert Museum. *Catalogue of an exhibition of Italian bronzes*. London 1961

Victoria and Albert Museum. *Catalogue of Italian plaquettes*. E. Maclagan. London 1924

Wallace Collection. *Catalogue of sculpture*. J. G. Mann. London 1931

Watson, W. *China before the Han Dynasty*. London 1961

Willetts, William. *Chinese Art*. London 1958

Woolley, Sir Leonard. *Ur of the Chaldees*. London 1929

Young, W. A. *Old English pattern books of the metal trades*. Victoria and Albert Museum. London 1913

Zervos, Christian. *L'art de la Mésopotamie*. Paris 1935

List of Illustrations

24 Horse of wrought bronze. Greek, *c.* 750 BC.

25 Bronze dagger-blade inlaid with gold, silver and niello, from Mycenae. L. $9\frac{3}{8}$ ins. National Museum, Athens.

26 Exterior of a kylix painted with scenes inside a bronze foundry. Greek, 5th century BC. From Vulci, now in Berlin. After Schreiber. Photo: Wilfred Walter.

27, 28 Bronze krater from Vix. Probably Greek, late 6th century BC. Musée de Chatillon-sur-Seine. Museum photo.

29 Banqueter. Probably Peloponnesian. Late 6th century BC. L. 4 ins. British Museum. Museum photo.

30 Girl running. Probably Spartan, *c.* 500 BC. H. $4\frac{1}{2}$ ins. British Museum. Museum photo.

31 Solid cast bronze statuette of a warrior on horseback. Greek, *c.* 550 BC. British Museum.

32 *Apollo of Piombino.* Greek, *c.* 500 BC. Louvre, Paris. Photo: Hirmer Verlag, Munich.

33 Medieval engraving of Helios, known as the Colossus of Rhodes.

34 The heroic statue of Zeus attributed to Calamis. Greek, 5th century BC. National Archaeological Museum, Athens. Photo: Alison Frantz, Athens.

35 The *Charioteer of Delphi*, *c.* 470 BC. Delphi Museum. Photo: Hirmer Verlag, Munich.

36 Griffin's head. From a cauldron. Greek, *c.* 630 BC. H. $9\frac{1}{4}$ ins. British Museum. Museum photo.

37 Bronze head of Hypnos (Sleep). Greek, late 4th century BC or a copy of Roman period. British Museum. Museum photo.

38 Fountain spout in the form of a dolphin. Roman, 1st century AD. British Museum.

39 Cast bronze of Aphrodite. Peloponnesian, 300–200 BC. British Museum.

40 Etruscan *biga* from Monteleone, 550–540 BC. Metropolitan Museum of Art, New York. Museum photo.

41 The *Chimera* of Arezzo. Etruscan, 4th century BC. Archaeological Museum, Florence. Photo: Mansell Collection.

42 The *Capitoline Wolf*. Etruscan, 6th century BC. Museo del Conservatori, Rome. Photo: Mansell Collection.

43 The *Orator*. Etruscan, 1st century BC. Archaeological Museum, Florence. Photo: Mansell Collection.

44 The equestrian statue of Marcus Aurelius, Piazza del Campidoglio, Rome. Photo: Fototeca Unione, Rome.

45 Mounted warrior, probably Alexander the Great. Roman, Imperial period. British Museum.

46 The bronze horses of St Mark's Venice. Photo: Mansell Collection.

47 Bronze horse from Herculaneum. Naples Museum. Photo: Mansell Collection.

48 Etruscan bucket with reliefs of Hercules and the Nemean lion, 400–300 BC. British Museum.

49 Aphrodite and Pan gaming. Incised bronze mirror-cover. Greek, 4th century BC. Diameter $7\frac{1}{4}$ ins. British Museum. Museum photo.

50 Polished bronze mirror. Greek, 450 BC. British Museum.

51 End supports of a couch. Roman, 1st century AD. British Museum.

52 Greek cuirass, 4th century BC. British Museum.

53 Gladiator's helmet. Roman, 2nd century AD. British Museum.

54 Greek helmet of the 5th century BC.

55 *Autumn* (Pomona). Imperial Roman period. British Museum.

56 *Pan*. Roman, 1st century AD. British Museum.

57 Part of a Roman water-pump. British Museum.

58 Heroic statue of the Emperor Theodosius or Heracleus. Barletta, probably 7th century. Photo: Hirmer Verlag, Munich.

59 The doors of Monte Cassino by the Byzantine bronze-founder Staurochios, 1066. Photo: Mansell Collection.

60 Bronze doors of St Bernward, Hildesheim Cathedral, 1015. Photo: Marburg.

61 Detail of *Ill. 60*. Adam and Eve before God. Photo: Marburg.

62 The Bernward Candlesticks. Magdalenenkirche, Hildesheim. Photo: Wehmeyer, Hildesheim.

63 Foot of a cross. Gilt bronze, 2nd half of the 11th century. Rhineland. H. 10¾ ins. Kestner Museum, Hannover. Museum photo.

64 The Gloucester Candlestick. Anglo-Norman. Victoria and Albert Museum. Museum photo.

65, 66 Milan candlestick, 12th century. Treasury of Milan Cathedral. Photos: Mansell Collection.

67 Equestrian aquamanile. English, *c.* 1300. British Museum. Museum photo.

68 *Simsonleuchter*. A pricket candlestick in brass in the form of Samson astride a lion. North German, 13th century. The Charlottenburg Museum, Berlin. Museum photo.

69 Aquamanile in the form of a centaur. German, 13th century. H. 14¼ ins. The Metropolitan Museum of Art, New York. Museum photo.

70 Bronze water-jug in the form of a seated lion. North German, 13th century. H. 7⅞ ins. Museum für Kunst und Gewerbe, Hamburg. Museum photo.

71 Head reliquary. Gilded bronze. German, 2nd half of the 12th century. H. 12⅜ ins. Kestner Museum, Hannover. Museum photo.

72 Baptismal font, 1220. Cathedral, Hildesheim. Photo: Marburg.

73 Bronze sanctuary door-knocker. Romanesque, 12th century. Durham Cathedral.

74 The bronze thurible of Godris. English, 10th–11th century. Photo: Sperryn's Limited, London.

75 Bronze mask. Nürnberg, end of 15th century. Germanisches Nationalmuseum, Nürnberg. Museum photo.

76 *Madonna*. Gilded bronze, perhaps from Hildesheim, 12th century. H. 15½ ins. Kestner Museum, Hannover. Museum photo.

77 Bronze piper from a fountain. German, *c.* 1380. Germanisches Nationalmuseum, Nürnberg. Museum photo.

78 Detail of the tomb of the Black Prince, Canterbury Cathedral, 14th century.

79 Altar tomb of the Earl of Warwick, Beauchamp Chapel, Warwick Castle.

80 Bronze bowl engraved with mythological subjects—Cadmus and the Labours of Hercules. English, 12th century. British Museum.

81 Bronze dish with Pelican motif. Dinant, *c.* 1480. Collection: Irwin Untermeyer, New York. Photo: Metropolitan Museum of Art, New York.

82 Reliquary of engraved and gilded copper, Abraham sacrificing Isaac. Lower Saxony, 11th–12th century. H. 3⅞ ins. Kestner Museum, Hannover. Museum photo.

83 Simon de Wensley. Rubbing of sepulchral brass at Wensley, Yorkshire. Late 14th century. British Museum. Museum photo.

84 Woodwose. Brass. German, 15th century. H. 8¼ ins. Victoria and Albert Museum. Museum photo.

85 Bronze *yü*. Shang dynasty. Hakutsuru Museum, Kobe.

86 Bronze *yü*. Shang dynasty. Musée Cernuschi, Paris. Museum photo.

87 Bronze *fang-yi*. Shang dynasty. Smithsonian Institution, Freer Gallery of Art, Washington DC.

88 Front of a recent slate box by the Haida people of the Canadian Pacific coast. After Boas.

89 Bronze *yü* in the shape of an owl. Shang-Yin dynasty. H. 6 ins. British Museum. Museum photo.

90 Bronze *tsun* in the form of an elephant. Shang dynasty. Musée Guimet, Paris. Photo: A. C. Cooper.

91 Pair of chariot lynch-pins. China, 9th–6th century BC. British Museum, Eumorfopoulos Collection. Museum photo.

92, 93 Gold and silver inlaid bronze chariot fittings. British Museum. Photo: Eileen Tweedy.

94 Table leg in animal form (one of a pair). Bronze inlaid with gold and silver. Late Chou dynasty. H. 4¾ ins. William Rockhill Nelson Gallery of Art, Kansas City. Museum photo.

95 Mongolian ponies. Late Chou dynasty. H. 8¼ ins. William Rockhill Nelson Gallery of Art, Kansas City. Museum photo.

96 Gilt bronze support in the shape of a bear. Han dynasty. British Museum.

97 Gilt bronze statue of Maitreya. Wel period. Metropolitan Museum of Art, New York. Museum photo.

98 Buddha. Romano-Buddhist. From Gandhara, 6th–7th century AD. Victoria and Albert Museum.

99 Chinese Buddhist group. Sui dynasty. Museum of Fine Arts, Boston. Museum photo.

100 Bronze sarcophagus. T'ang dynasty. H. 14⅜ ins. Freer Gallery of Art, Washington DC. Museum photo.

101 Bronze openwork mount, from the Caucasus. Scythian, *c.* 5th century BC. L. 5½ ins. British Museum. Museum photo.

102 Pole-finial. Ibex head. Sino-Siberian, 5th–1st century BC. Museum of Fine Arts, Boston. Museum photo.

103 Bronze ibex. Sino-Siberian, 5th–1st century BC. Museum of Fine Arts, Boston. Museum photo.

104 Pole-finial. Elk. Chinese, Han dynasty. British Museum. Photo: Edwin Smith.

105 Bronze figure of a lion inlaid with gold and silver. Chinese, Sung dynasty. British Museum. Museum photo.

106 The Buddha of Healing. Gilt bronze. Late 7th century AD. H. 101 ins. From Nara, Japan.

107 The Great Buddha, Kamakura. Japan, 13th century. Photo: Japan National Tourist Organization.

108 Bronze hunting group. Primitive Indian village work. Probably 19th century. Victoria and Albert Museum. Museum photo.

109 Hanuman, from a Vaishnara shrine. Ceylon, 11th century or later. Victoria and Albert Museum. Museum photo.

110 *Siva Nataraja*. Madras, *c.* 12th century. Victoria and Albert Museum. Museum photo.

111 Standard-head. Luristan, *c.* 6th century BC. British Museum. Museum photo.

112 Head of an ibex. Furniture-mount. Persian, Achaemenid period. 6th–5th century BC. British Museum. Museum photo.

113 Bridle-piece. Luristan, *c.* 500 BC. British Museum. Museum photo.

114 Bronze bust of a Sasanian king. Persian, 6th–7th century. Louvre, Paris. Photo: Brompton studio.

115 Inlaid brass ewer, made in Mosul, 1232. North Mesopotamian. H. 12 ins. British Museum. Museum photo.

116 Andrea Pisano. Southern doors, Baptistery, Florence, 1330–36. Photo: Mansell Collection.

117 Detail of *Ill. 116*. Photo: Mansell Collection.

118 Detail of *Ill. 119*. Photo: Brogi.

119 Lorenzo Ghiberti. Northern doors, Baptistery, Florence, 1404–24. Photo: Brogi.

120 Ghiberti. *John the Baptist brought before Herod*. Panel from the Baptistery Font, Siena. Completed 1425. Photo: Mansell Collection.

121 Ghiberti. Panel from the Eastern doors, Baptistery, Florence, 1425–52. Photo: Mansell Collection.

122 Donatello. *St Louis of Toulouse*. Gilded Bronze, *c.* 1423. Museo S. Croce, Florence. Photo: Mansell Collection.

123 Donatello. *David*, *c.* 1430. Bargello, Florence. Photo: Brogi.

124 Donatello. *Herod's Feast*, 1423–27. Baptistery Font, Siena. Photo: Brogi.

125 Donatello. Arguing figures from door of Sacristy of San Lorenzo, Florence, 1435–39. Photo: Alinari, Florence.

126 Donatello. Gattamelata. Piazza del Santo, Padua. Photo: Brogi.

127 Detail of *Ill. 126*. Photo: Anderson, Rome.

128 Detail of *Ill. 126*. Photo: Anderson, Rome.

129 Andrea Verrocchio. Bartolommeo Colleone. Venice, 1479–88. Photo: Anderson, Rome.

130 Leonardo da Vinci. Study of a horseman. Drawing. Probably a study for the Sforza monument. Milan period 1483–90. Royal Collection, Windsor.

,1 Putto with a Fish. Workshop of Donatello. Florentine, 2nd quarter of 15th century. H. 15 ins. Victoria and Albert Museum. Museum photo.

132 Francesco di Giorgio Martini. *Young Bacchante*, *c.* 1500. Kunsthistorisches Museum, Vienna. Museum photo.

133 Andrea del Verrocchio. *David*. Before 1476. Bargello, Florence. Photo: Alinari.

134 Bertholdo da Giovanni. *Bellerophon and Pegasus*, *c.* 1483. H. $12\frac{3}{4}$ ins. Kunsthistorisches Museum, Vienna. Museum photo.

135, 136 Pair of female grotesques, 16th century. Staatliche Museen, Berlin, Museum photos.

137 *Satyr*. Workshop of Riccio. Padua, early 16th century. Staatliche Museen, Berlin. Museum photo.

138 Riccio. *Boy struggling with a goose*. Early 16th century. Kunsthistorisches Museum, Vienna. Museum photo.

139 Riccio. Lamp in the form of a grotesque monster. Early 16th century.

140 Riccio. *Mounted warrior*. Padua, early 16th century. H. $13\frac{1}{4}$ ins. Victoria and Albert Museum. Museum photo.

141 Riccio. Paschal candlestick, Basilica of San Antonio, Padua, 1507–15. Photo: Alinari.

142 Benvenuto Cellini. *Perseus*, 1554. Loggia dei Lanzi, Florence. Photo: Alinari.

143 Cellini. *Head of Medusa*. Victoria and Albert Museum. Museum photo.

144 Cellini. Cosimo I de' Medici. Bargello, Florence. Photo: Alinari.

145 Cellini. *Ganymede mounted on Zeus*. Bargello, Florence. Photo: Mansell Collection.

146 Antonio Pollaiolo. *Hercules and Anteus*, *c.* 1475–80. Bargello, Florence. Photo: Mansell Collection.

147 *Hercules and the Nemean Lion*. Florentine. Early 16th century. Victoria and Albert Museum. Museum photo.

148 Giovanni da Bologna. *The Rape of the Sabine*, 1579–83. Kuntshistorisches Museum, Vienna. Museum photo.

149 After Giovanni da Bologna. *Virtue triumphing over Vice*, 2nd half of 16th century. Wallace Collection. Museum photo.

150 Giovanni da Bologna. *Astronomy*. Gilded bronze. Kunsthistorisches Museum, Vienna. Museum photo.

151 Giovanni da Bologna. *Mercury*, 1580. Bargello, Florence. Photo: Mansell Collection.

152 Leone Lione. *Charles V*. Kunsthistorisches Museum, Vienna. Museum photo.

153 Adriaen de Vries, Mercury fountain, Augsburg. Completed 1599. Photo: Peter Cannon-Brookes.

154 Jacopo Tatti (Sansovino). *Jupiter*. Kunsthistorisches Museum, Vienna. Museum photo.

155 Germaine Pilon. *Charles IX of France*, 2nd half of 16th century. Wallace Collection. Museum photo.

156 Cellini. *The Nymph of Fontainebleau*, 1543. Louvre, Paris. Photo: Giraudon.

157 Peter Vischer and his sons. Sebaldusgrab (Shrine of St Sebaldus). Bronze 1488–1519. St Sebaldus, Nürnberg. Photo: Marburg.

158 Detail of *Ill. 157*. Photo: Helga Schmidt-Glassner, Stuttgart.

159 Bronze lion originally intended for the Sebaldusgrab. Germanisches Nationalmuseum, Nürnberg. Museum photo.

160 Detail of *Ill. 157*. Peter Vischer's self-portrait. Photo: Paul Janke, Nürnberg.

161 Detail of *Ill. 162*.

162 The Tomb of the Holy Roman Emperor, Maximilian I. Hofkirche, Innsbruck.

163 Pancraz Labenwolf. Limewood model for the *Gänsemännchen*, 16th century. Germanisches Nationalmuseum, Nürnbérg. Museum photo.

164 Detail of *Ill. 162*.

165 Peter Flötner. *Apollo and Daphne*, *c.* 1540. Nürnberg. Germanisches Nationalmuseum, Nürnberg. Museum photo.

166 Konrad Veit. *Mars and Venus*, *c.* 1525. Germanisches Nationalmuseum, Nürnberg. Museum photo.

167 Limewood model for the handle of a vase in either gold or bronze. Probably Nürnberg, *c.* 1580. Staatliche Museen, Berlin. Museum photo.

168 Pietro Torregiano. Tomb of Henry VII and his Consort Elizabeth of York. Westminster Abbey.

169 Wentzel Jamnitzer and J. G. van der Schardt. *Spring*. Gilded bronze. H. 30 ins. Kunsthistorisches Museum, Vienna. Museum photo.

170 Pietro Tacca. Inkstand. First quarter of the 17th century. Victoria and Albert Museum. Museum photo.

171 Giovanni Lorenzo Bernini. *Baldacchino*. St Peter's, Rome, 1624–33. Photo: Gabinetto Fotografico Nazionale, Rome.

172 Bernini. Tomb of Pope Alexander VII. St Peter's Rome, 1671–78. Photo: Mansell Collection.

173 Alessandro Algardi. Pope Innocent X. Begun 1645. Palazzo del Conservatori, Rome. Photo: Mansell Collection.

174 Girardon. Louis Quatorze. A reduction (H. 17¼ ins.). Wallace Collection. Museum photo.

175 Girardon. Vase. A bronze reduction of one of a pair of marble vases. Wallace Collection. Museum photo.

176 After Gian da Bologna. Henri Quatre, King of France. Franco-Italian, early 17th century. Wallace Collection. Museum photo.

177 The River Nile. French, 2nd half of the 17th century. Wallace Collection. Museum photo.

178 Massimiliano Soldani. *Faun*. Bargello, Florence. Photo: Mansell Collection.

179 Girardon. *Pluto carrying off Proserpine*, 1693. H. 21 ins. Wallace Collection. Museum photo.

180 Louis-Simon Boizot. *Pluto carrying off Proserpine*, 18th century. Wallace Collection. Museum photo.

181 Detail of the corner-piece of a *commode*.

182 Wall-light. French, mid-18th century. Wallace Collection. Museum photo.

183 After Houdon. *Le Baiser donné*. H. 4½ ins. Wallace Collection. Museum photo.

184 After Houdon. *Le Baiser rendu*. Wallace Collection. Museum photo.

185 Etienne-Maurice Falconet. *Peter the Great*, *c.* 1766–79. Leningrad.

186 Guillaune I Coustou. Contemporary bronze reduction of one of the marble horses for the Marly riding-school, 1740–45. Wallace Collection. Museum photo.

187 The Avignon Clock by Gouthière after Boizot. Wallace Collection. Museum photo.

188 Virgin and Child. Gilded bronze. Italian, Bologna, *c.* 1750. Victoria and Albert Museum. Museum photo.

189 Antoine-Louis Barye. *Jaguar devouring an alligator*. Ny Carlsberg Glyptotek, Copenhagen.

190 Auguste Rodin. *The Age of Bronze*, 1877. H. 72¼ ins. Wallraf-Richartz-Museum, Cologne. Photo: Rheinisches Bildarchiv.

191 Auguste Rodin. *La Porte d'Enfer*. Rodin Museum, Paris. Photo: Bulloz, Paris.

192 Auguste Rodin. *Le Baiser*. Bronze version. H. 23½ ins. Photo: Parke-Bernet Galleries Inc., New York.

193 Edgar Degas. *Dancer*. Landesmuseum, Hannover. Museum photo.

194 Honoré Daumier. *Ratapoil*. Photo: Sotheby & Co.

195 Aristide Maillol. *Torso*, 1905–6. H. 48 ins. Tate Gallery. Museum photo.

196 Pierre-Auguste Renoir. *La petite laveuse accroupie* (*Water* from a set of four representing the elements), *c.* 1917–18. H. 13¼ ins. Kunsthaus Lempertz. Photo: Rheinisches Bildarchiv, Cologne.

197 Gilt-bronze lamp, probably after Paul Roche. French, *c.* 1900. Photo: Sotheby & Co., London.

198 George Frederic Watts. *Clytie*, *c.* 1868–80. H. 33 ins. Tate Gallery. Museum photo.

199 Sir Jacob Epstein. *Kitty*. Photo: Sotheby & Co., London.

200 Georges Braque. *Cheval*, 1939. Photo: Parke-Bernet Galleries Inc., New York.

201 Henri Matisse. *Deux Négresses*, 1908. Photo: Sotheby & Co., London.

202 Pablo Picasso. *Buste d'une femme*, 1905. Bronze. H. 16 ins. Photo: Brassaï, Paris.

203 Ossip Zadkine, *Standing Woman*, 1920.

204 Jacques Lipchitz, *Guitar Player*, 1918. H. 28⅜ ins. Stadt Kunstmuseum, Duisburg.

205 Marino Marini. *Horse and Rider*, 1947. H. 63½ ins. Tate Callery. Photo: F. L. Kenett.

206 Henry Moore. *Warrior with Shield*, 1953–54. H. 60 ins. Toronto Art Gallery, Canada. Photo: the artist.

207 Wilhelm Lehmbruck. *Young Man Seated*, 1918. H. 41 ins. Stadt Kunstmuseum, Duisburg.

208 Germaine Richier. *The Wasp*, 1953. Galerie Creuzevault, Paris.

209 Jean Arp. *Ptolomy I*, 1953. H. 40½ ins. Mr and Mrs William Mazer, New York.

Index